A COMMONSENSE APPROACH TO THE BOOK OF REVELATION

MARIE STRONG
with a study guide by Sharon Clark Pearson

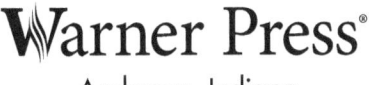

Anderson, Indiana

Copyright © 1996 by Warner Press. First edition copyright © 1980 by Warner Press under the title *Basic Teachings from Patmos*. All rights reserved. No part of this publication may be reproduced, stored in a retrieval system, or transmitted in any form or by any means—electronic, mechanical, photocopy, recording or any other—except for brief quotations in printed reviews, without prior written permission of the publisher. For this and all other editorial matters, please contact the Publishing Assistant at the address below. To purchase additional copies of this book, to inquire about distribution, and for all other sales-related matters, please contact the Sales Department at:

Warner Press, Inc.
PO Box 2499
Anderson, IN 46018-2499
800-741-7721
www.warnerpress.org

All Scripture quotations, unless otherwise indicated, are taken from the Holy Bible, New International Version®. NIV®. Copyright © 1973, 1978, 1984 by International Bible Society. Used by permission of Zondervan. All rights reserved.

Scripture quotations marked NRSV are taken from New Revised Standard Version Bible, copyright 1989, Division of Christian Education of the National Council of the Churches of Christ in the United States of America. Used by permission. All rights reserved.

Cover design by Mike Baker
Text design by Curtis D. Corzine
Content editing by Sharon Clark Pearson
Copyediting by Stephen R. Lewis

ISBN-13: 978-087162676-9

Printed in the United States of America.

POD—LSI

TABLE OF CONTENTS

Editor's Preface to the Second Edition i
Preface to the First Edition iii

1. Symbolic Writing 1
2. The Seven Churches of Asia (Rev 1–3) 7
3. An Open Door and a Scroll (Rev 4–5) 11
4. The Opening of the Scrolls (Rev 6–7) 17
5. The Woes of the Seven Trumpets (Rev 8–11) 23
6. The Woman, the Dragon, and the Beast (Rev 12–14) 27
7. The Seven Bowls (Rev 15–16) 39
8. Judgment on the Empire (Rev 17–18) 43
9. The Triumph of Christ (Rev 19: 1–22:5) 47
10. The Epilogue and Conclusion (Rev 22:6–21) 57

Appendix A: Glossary of Symbols 61
Appendix B: Recapitulation Defined and Illustrated 63
Appendix C: Satan Cast Out (Rev 12:7–12) 65
Bibliography 67

Study Guide by Sharon Clark Pearson 69

EDITOR'S PREFACE TO THE SECOND EDITION

In the fall of 1994, Dr. Marie Strong called me; she was excited to share the delightful news that her book *Basic Teachings from Patmos* was to be reprinted with her revision under the title *A Commonsense Approach to the Book of Revelation*. She asked if I might be willing to reread it and make suggestions to her. I agreed even though I was not sure that my help would be needed at all!

We spoke the last time just before I left for a trip to the Holy Land on January 2, 1995. She said, "Now Sharon, you are going to have to be stalwart" and proceeded to give me an update on a new reversal in her health. I assured Marie of my love and prayers. As I hung up the telephone, I had no idea that she would not completely finish her book, nor did I realize I was saying my last good-bye to her.

I was appointed the responsibility of finishing Marie's book, and several months later I dared to open her carefully organized drafts; even the first drafts of the first edition were there! She had almost completed her final draft of this revised edition; all that was left was follow-through on some handwritten directions and notes about revision that was left to do. So my part in the presentation of this book was minimal. As I interpreted her handwriting and her directions, I thanked God for this little book, so powerful in its simplicity and clarity! I blessed God for this woman who had lived among us with such grace and wisdom.

Marie is now a part of that great cloud of witnesses that inspires us to persevere by looking to Jesus (Hebrews 12:1–2). This book is the legacy of Dr. Marie Strong to the church. Thanks be to God!

And thank you, Marie!
Sharon Clark Pearson

PREFACE TO THE FIRST EDITION

Why another treatise on the book of Revelation? The market is flooded with such books. Many and varied are the notions about the future. Much that is said about religion today seems to come right out of the book of Revelation. That is precisely why I write this little book. The opinions have been many and the conclusions too weird. The basic message John tried to write got lost somewhere in a morass of speculation that must puzzle even the angels in the book of Revelation.

This does not pretend to be a commentary, or even an average-size book. I have tried, first of all, to give a very brief explanation of Apocalyptic writing. An attempt was made to see the historical situation that caused John to write. As little as possible was done with the symbols. I sincerely tried to see the basic message and its application to the people John was seeking to help. Since I believe the Bible to be God's word to humans, it was necessary, at least to me, to find the core or eternal truth that applies to all people and all ages. I sincerely believe the message from Patmos is relevant and one the church of the twentieth century needs. This was and is my aim. This little book is intended as a guide to an understanding of the message John gave to the church. For full understanding, the book of Revelation must be read together with this little guide. Anyone who has the Spirit of God can understand God's word, for "the Spirit searches all things, even the deep things of God" (1 Cor 2:10).

Marie Strong

1
SYMBOLIC WRITING

The book of Revelation seems very different from other biblical books. It is a book full of angels doing strange things, of beasts, of dragons, of the earth opening its mouth and swallowing rivers. Living creatures speak and horses of varied colors gallop across the pages of history. What is the meaning of this peculiar book, or does it have a meaning? Is it, as one scholar has suggested, the wild ravings of the mad man from Patmos? Why is such a strange book in the Bible? What meaning could it possibly have for us?

There are many and varied opinions regarding the meaning of this book. Generally speaking, these opinions can be grouped into four categories:

1. The Futurist View: The entire book of Revelation relates to the future, to a millennial or one thousand year reign of Christ on earth.
2. The Preterist View: This is almost the opposite view from the above. It holds that all the events in the book have taken place in past history.
3. The Historical View: According to this position, some of the events have already taken place while others are still to be fulfilled in history.
4. The Spiritual Interpretation: This position disregards history entirely and gives the whole book of Revelation a spiritual meaning.

A COMMONSENSE APPROACH TO...REVELATION

There is such a diversity of opinion regarding the meaning of this book that thinking Christians tend to disregard it and omit it from their devotional reading.

It is not necessary to give up, as most Christians do, any attempt at understanding the book. What is necessary is an understanding of proper methods of interpretation. To understand or properly interpret any book, biblical or otherwise, one must try to understand why the author writes as he or she does. What is going on at the time he or she is writing?

If we look back in the Old Testament, we will see other books, such as Ezekiel and Daniel, also written in this same way. Daniel has a number of peculiar animals, and Ezekiel writes of dry dead bones coming back together and becoming alive, of wheels inside of wheels moving through the air. Are all of these writers writing nonsense, or is there meaning in the writing?

We have said that to understand any book, we must understand the situation at the time the writer is writing. Ezekiel plainly says he is writing during the Babylonian captivity. The Jewish nation had been conquered by Babylonia. Many Jews began worshiping the gods of the Babylonians. Since the temple had been destroyed and God lived in the temple, the Jews wondered if God also had been destroyed. For many years, people believed that during any war, gods fought for their devotees; whichever nation won had the strongest god. There were probably many Jews who believed that the Babylonian god was superior to their own God. Ezekiel speaks to that situation.

The book of Daniel does not give a date. The scholars have arrived at fairly exact dating by studying the types of language used in the book. At the time Daniel was written, Antiochus Epiphanes was persecuting the Jewish people. His laws almost completely suppressed all Jewish religious practices. Many Jews gave up their faith rather than be killed. Jews were killed for owning a copy of their scriptures, for attending worship, or for

1 SYMBOLIC WRITINGS

keeping the Sabbath. Many, even among the priests, gave up their religion to avoid death. The writer of the book of Daniel writes to save the faith of Israel. This event is described in 1 Maccabees in the Apocrypha.

Since it was dangerous to write plainly, the writers of these unusual books wrote in symbols. This would be very similar to modern wartime when danger requires intelligence units of the army to write in code. Only those who know the key to the code can understand or read the writing. The Jewish people developed such a system; it was called Apocalyptic writing. The result of the writing, or the book itself, was called an Apocalypse. The word means that something hidden is now made known or revealed. Thus the book of Revelation is often called the Apocalypse.

Apocalypses were written during times of persecution or danger in order to encourage the people of God so that they would not give up their religion. The writers do this by showing that God's kingdom will triumph over evil. In all Revelations or Apocalypses, good and evil are in combat, but good wins. Everything in history is under the control of God. Since the writer writes during a period of extreme danger, he must disguise his statements. He frequently does this by the use of people or events of the past, for he does not dare use the name of the present rulers. Thus, if the persecuting rulers find the book, it appears to be nonsense to them. When the people of God read the book, they are encouraged because the book shows that the evil rulers over them will soon be destroyed, that God's people will be preserved, that God's kingdom is triumphant.

The book of Daniel does not name the Greek rulers but takes a ruler of the past, the Babylonian king, Nebuchadnezzar, as the evil force whose kingdom will soon end. One should not look for historical accuracy in such books, because they are not books of history. They are books written in code in order to preserve God's people and God's truth.

Neither are such books, books of prophecy of some great reign of Christ on earth someday. Nor does Ezekiel describe the modern airplane or automobile. He is writing in symbols or code in order to hide his meaning from the persecutors. He is probably showing by his strange wheels inside of wheels, which go in all directions, that God can get around, that God can even get over to Babylonia and be with his people who are captives there. The Jews of Ezekiel's time believed God lived only in the temple in Jerusalem. When the temple was destroyed, they believed God had been defeated. Ezekiel wrote to that situation.

The Bible is not just any book; it is inspired by God and therefore has meaning for people in every age. Its message is as relevant today as when first written. If Apocalyptic literature such as Ezekiel, Daniel, and Revelation were written for a crisis at the time the writers lived, how can it apply to us today? In all Scripture, even Apocalyptic writing, there is an eternal truth that is as up-to-date as this morning's newspaper. This core or kernel of truth runs throughout Scripture, and the follower of God must find it. What is the core or kernel of truth in Apocalyptic writing? It is that God always cares about his people, that God will triumph over evil. Evil may seem to win. If someone mistreats you because you are a Christian, you are to rejoice and be exceedingly glad, for great is your reward in heaven (Matt 5:12). Even if you are killed for your faith, you will still live with Christ forever. All the way through the book of Revelation, Christians are suffering and being killed for their faith. They are encouraged to cling to their faith and continue to believe because God and good will win. The beast (evil) in Revelation 13 will be destroyed in the lake of fire, but God's people will reign forever and ever. God cares and will lead the flock like a shepherd and gather them from all the places where they are scattered (Ezek 34). They will be taken to an eternal home and will live forever. God really cares. "He will wipe every tear from their eyes. There will be no more death or mourning

1 SYMBOLIC WRITINGS

or crying or pain" (Rev 21:4). With a message like that, is it any wonder that the book of Revelation has become the favorite of people in prison and concentration camps throughout the world?

The major ideas in Apocalyptic literature are these:

1. God rules over all of history.
2. Evil and good are in constant conflict.
3. God and good will win.
4. God cares about the people of God and reveals the truth to them even in the midst of danger.

If one keeps these major ideas in mind as one reads the book of Revelation, even that seemingly mysterious book will make good sense. Furthermore, it will be a real encouragement in the small and great battles of life.

It is very easy to see that in the book of Revelation Christians are being persecuted and killed for their faith. But just who is doing the persecuting, the killing? The writer of Revelation does not say but gives some hints. He calls the persecuting force "the dragon" (Rev 12) and "the beast" (Rev 13). This force had power and authority (v 2); "the whole world was astonished and followed the beast…they also worshiped the beast" (vv 3–4).

About the only authority with power in the first century was the Roman Empire. Nero persecuted the church, but only in the city of Rome. The events in the book of Revelation take place in Asia Minor, called Asia in the first century. The cities of Asia or that area are named in the first chapters of the book of Revelation. In Revelation, emperor worship is the major issue (note e.g., Rev 13:4, 12–15). Christians were killed for failure to worship the image of the beast. This does not fit Nero. He killed Christians, to be sure, but because he blamed them for the fire in Rome. There is no historical evidence of required emperor worship during the reign of Nero.

The emperor Tragan (AD 111–16) killed Christians, but his dates are too late to fit much of the book of Revelation. Later emperors persecuted Christians to death, and the catacombs are grim evidence of that slaughter. The very basic beliefs of Christianity are opposed to the pagan practices of the Roman Empire. Christians preached peace; Rome lived by war. Christians preached humility; Rome lived arrogance. Christians lived and taught love, even to enemies; Rome's very life depended upon conquest of the enemy. Christians worshiped one God who made heaven and earth; Rome demanded the worship of many gods. Christians' failure to worship the gods of Rome made them suspect. They were considered atheists because they refused to worship the gods. From the very beginning, the two systems, Roman paganism and Christianity, were on a collision course. The book of Revelation is the picture of a part of that drama. The writer, John, sees this conflict already taking shape. He is apparently writing during the reign of Domitian who demanded to be worshiped. All who failed to respond were killed. The Christians seemed to be his major target. John sees the conflict continuing beyond his own time but promises the Christians that final victory is with God and that evil will one day be destroyed in the lake of fire.

The principles that brought the persecution of early Christianity are still at war against God's people. The forces of evil take different names and shapes in the various periods of history, but their basic motivations are always satanic and, therefore, always at war with God's people. No accommodation, no appeasement or compromise, is ever possible between good and evil, between God and Satan. We need to be constantly growing in our sensitivity to God so that we recognize the evil forces that try to subdue us.

2
THE SEVEN CHURCHES OF ASIA

Revelation 1–3

The first words of the book of Revelation show that it is the revelation of Jesus Christ. John may be the writer, but Jesus is the true author, and an angel delivers the message to John. This gives the book eternal authority. A special blessing is promised to those who recognize that authority by reading and keeping the words in the book (Rev 1:1–3).

The very first part of the book (Rev 1:4–9) shows the authority of God and of Jesus Christ. Jesus is still on his throne. He is Alpha and Omega—the beginning and end of all things. He will one day come in clouds of glory and even the evil powers will see him. This same One, who will one day come on the clouds, appears to John.

He is described in many Apocalyptic terms in 1:4–16. He is the same one who died for us and was resurrected (Rev 1:17–18).

In 1:4, John says he is writing to the seven churches of Asia. What is today Turkey was the Asia John was referring to from its ancient name, Asia Minor. These are symbolized by seven stars and seven lampstands. There were certainly more than seven churches at the time John was writing, so why does he just refer to seven? In Hebrew Apocalyptic, seven was a sacred number meaning completeness. Jesus used that same number when he told Peter he was not only to forgive seven times but seventy times seven or forgive completely and always (Matt 18:21–22). From this perspective, John, as any true prophet, is writing to his time. The seven churches were existing during John's lifetime. Since Scripture has a meaning for all time, one could make a comparison between the seven and churches today. The seven churches are all churches everywhere and in all times in history. They are your congregation and mine. The angels of the churches known by John are the leaders or pastors. The message is directed at those leaders or pastors, possibly because any group of people rarely rises above its leadership.

Some congregations, like Ephesus, have lost their first love (their conversion experience). They must repent or their lampstand will be removed (Rev 2:4–5). Jesus referred to a lampstand in Matthew 5:15. Christians were to let their light shine—not put it under a bushel, but on a lampstand so that it would shine before everyone. The lampstand is probably the Christian influence of the church that will be taken away unless they repent. Isn't it very true that if Christians do not live like Christ, their Christian influence dies? The church at Ephesus had one virtue, however; they hated the work of the Nicolaitans (Rev 2:6). The Nicolaitans were gnostic in their thinking. Their basic belief was that good and evil were so opposed to each other that they could never meet. So God who was eternal good could not have created the world that was material and evil. Christ, who was good, could not have become human because humans are basically evil and Christ is eternal good. The church in Ephesus hated this false doctrine. It is good to hate false doctrine, but any church can get so carried away by its concern for pure doctrine that it will lose sight of the people and of God. Thus, it will lose its first love.

Smyrna is the only city of the seven John writes to that is still in existence today (modern Izmir). Some congregations are like Smyrna (Rev 2:8–11), who have suffered much persecution but are still true to God. They have recognized those who profess to be Christians but are not. Notice that the writer uses the word *Jews* for Christians as Paul sometimes does. See for example, Galatians 3:29; 4:27–28, or Romans 2:29, which says, "A person is a Jew who is one inwardly, and real circumcision is a matter of the heart" (NRSV). The writer of Revelation calls Christians Jews because he would not dare use the term Christian without endangering the lives of those Christians he was trying to help.

Some congregations are like Pergamum (Rev 2:12–17), who allow false doctrine (the Nicolaitans) to exist and lead people astray. At one time the congregation had been faithful, for one of them (Antipas, probably an Apocalyptic name for a Christian) was killed for his faith. The congregation is to repent of their acceptance of false doctrine (Balaam and the Nicolaitans).

Some congregations are like the church in Thyatira (Rev 2:18–29). They have love and faith, service and patience, but they are mixed up with evil. Morris reminds us that the longest of the seven letters was written to the smallest town, Thyatira. Morris quotes Sir William Ramsey[1] who said that in John's time Thyatira had a number of trade guilds (similar to unions of our time). Luke mentions Thyatira in his description of Lydia (Acts 16:14), a seller of purple dye, who was from that town. Emperor worship was so strong in Thyatira that the trade guilds required attendance at guild banquets where the meat that was served had been offered to idols.[2] Also, these banquets often resulted in the "sexual looseness" of those present (Morris 71). The Jezebel mentioned professed the Christian faith and

---

1. Sir William Ramsey was an archaeologist who traveled to the Middle East in the early 1900s to prove the New Testament gave false information regarding history. Ramsey returned home a true believer in Christianity because of what he learned. He wrote a number of books about that which convinced him of the truth of the Bible.

2. The problem of eating meat that was connected to idol worship was a problem the apostle Paul had to address in the Corinthian church (1 Corinthians, chapters 8 and 10).

claimed to be a church leader—a prophet. The failure of the church is that they tolerate this one who is teaching the evil doctrine that adopting the mind of paganism wasn't so bad. In that day, since belonging to the guilds was expected for those employed in a trade, it is easy to see how attractive this bit of sin became. There is an eternal message here, for every Christian has to continually decide where to draw the line between true Christian conduct and adherence to the world's standards. Even in today's world, failure to "go along with the crowd" often means failure to climb the ladder of success on the job.

The writer of Revelation warns the congregation at Thyatira. They will be called to account for their works, either toleration of the evil one or the doctrine she taught, which the writer calls "the deep things of Satan" (v 24 NRSV). Those who have been beguiled by such teaching are warned to repent. Furthermore, a prophecy of doom is given against this leader—a warning for all who continue to consort with her. Those in the congregation who have not been led astray are encouraged to continue their faith and will be rewarded.

Other congregations are like Sardis (Rev 3:1–6); they have a reputation for being alive but are dead. These are to repent. There are some in the congregation who are worthy. They walk with Christ in white (purity), and their names will not be blotted out of the Book of Life.

Some congregations are like Philadelphia (Rev 3:7–13). They are small and have a great influence in the world but have kept Christ's word and are true to him. Other churches, even the synagogue of Satan, a possible reference to the church in Pergamum, will see their great works and will come to value them (bow down to them).

Many churches, sad to say, are like the church in Laodicea. They are lukewarm, neither cold nor hot (Rev 3:15–22). These God spits out of his mouth. They say they are rich and need nothing. They don't realize they are poor. They must repent and buy true gold from God.

3
AN OPEN DOOR AND A SCROLL

Revelation 4–5

After John has spoken to specific problems in the seven churches of Asia, he begins in earnest to tell the future events. From chapter 4 on, events follow one another in rapid succession almost like a stage play. It is really a mystery drama, for the writer gives one clue after another to help his audience understand the major theme. The characters, some very weird ones, appear upon John's stage but all tell the same general story. Although the characters differ or the symbols change, they depict the major central message John is trying to tell. This method of repeating the same message but using different symbols is called recapitulation. An illustration of this principle is given in Appendix B.

John doesn't immediately give his major point, for like a good mystery writer, he keeps his readers in suspense.

In 4:1, John sees the door standing open in heaven. Since he is writing in symbols or code, it cannot be a literal door. The last part of the verse explains that the door is the revelation of what is to come. God is going to let John in on the mystery or the secret of his plan for the future of the earth. This mystery, God, through John, will reveal to the church, but it will be hidden from those outside the church.

The idea of God revealing truth to his people and that truth remaining a mystery to outsiders is mentioned elsewhere in the New Testament (e.g., Eph 3:4–5). Also notice the words of Jesus to his disciples, "The knowledge of the secrets of the kingdom of heaven has been given to you, but not to them" (Matt 13:11). A special secret or mystery is to be revealed to John as it was to the Old Testament prophets (notice Is 8:16). John's spiritual eyes see what is to happen in the future. He sees a throne in heaven (4:2). Like Isaiah's vision in Isaiah 6, the throne seems to mean the absolute power of God. The One seated on the throne resembles jasper and carnelian. Carnelian, or sardius, is a precious gem possibly imported from Arabia or India. This sounds much like Ezekiel's description of God (see Ezek 1:26–28). In place of Ezekiel's amber and fire or bronze, John uses jasper and carnelian. Both writers are probably trying to show that God is high above humankind, as in Isaiah 6. This was the original meaning of the term *holy*. The attribute of holiness meant that God was above or apart from humans, or different from them. The rainbow all around God reminds us of the Noah story in Genesis 11: 12–13, where the rainbow shows God's covenant with humanity, probably meaning God's patience and long-suffering toward evil society. It was also a promise for the future.

It is not certain what the elders signify (4:4). Some take them to mean angels; others believe they represent human power. According to Metzger, "these Elders may represent the twelve patriarchs of the Old Testament and the twelve apostles of the New Testament, symbolizing the two covenants of the people of God."[1] Their identity is possibly unimportant. The crowns show that they represent authority of some kind. That is all that is necessary for us to understand. The flashes of lightning and blasts of thunder are reminiscent of Mount Sinai and the giving of the law to Moses (see Exodus 19:16). Usually in Apocalyptic, thunder and lightning show God's power.

The Little Apocalypse talks about the powers of heaven being shaken (Matt 24:29). (The Little Apocalypse is a phrase used to describe Matthew 24, Luke 21, and Mark 13 where

---

1. Metzger, *Breaking the Code*, 49.

3 AN OPEN DOOR AND A SCROLL

Jesus foretells the destruction of Jerusalem and the end of the world.) A similar image is used by Joel in 2:30–31 and then quoted by Peter on the day of Pentecost (Acts 2:19–20) when the crowd asked the meaning of "the rushing mighty wind and the tongues of fire." It all shows God's power to create, to destroy, to break into history at any time God wills. The rainbow at this point may have reminded the church that God is as capable of destroying wicked humanity as he was in Noah's time. The rainbow was also a promise of a new beginning for God's people. One should not get lost in the symbols and miss the major point. This is often done and is probably straining out a gnat and swallowing a camel (Matt 23:24).

The four living creatures, lion, ox, eagle, and human were well-known symbols in Hebrew thought. They sound like the cherubim or the seraphim of the Old Testament (Ezek 1 and Is 6:2). Human beings were considered the greatest of all creations, the lion the greatest of the animals, and the eagle represented the greatest among the birds.[2] The eyes everywhere seem to say the animals had all knowledge. Since this is Apocalyptic, these are all symbols of creation itself. When they say, "Holy, holy, holy, Lord God Almighty," they show that they have power based on perfect knowledge of God's greatness and his deserved honor (4:9–10). This causes the elders, representing all human authority, to bow down and worship the one who is on the throne (v 11). This all reminds one of Paul's words in Philippians 2:9–11, where he says, "Therefore God exalted him to the highest place and gave him the name that is above every name, that at the name of Jesus every knee should bow, in heaven and on earth and under the earth, and every tongue confess that Jesus Christ is Lord, to the glory of God the Father." Ultimately, all power in heaven and earth will be silent before and subject to God. For a description of the powers and Jesus' relation to them, see Colossians 1:15–20 and 2:8–15.

---

2. Kiddle, *Revelation*, 90–91.

The Scroll and the Lamb
Revelation 5

Chapter 5 is a continuation of the events in chapter 4, and the two should be read as one story. The scroll with writing on it is also found in Ezekiel 2:11. The scroll will tell the story of the destiny of the world and God's plan for the future, given in detail, that is, written on the back as well as the inside. The seals are a usual part of Apocalyptic whose message is hidden or sealed until revealed to one of God's servants. The seven, again, means complete. No one is able to open the scroll, which distresses John to the point of his weeping. Finally, one of the elders notes that the Lion of Judah's tribe has earned the right to open the scroll. The Messiah or Christ, being of the tribe of Judah, was a well-known figure among the Hebrew people, as we see in Isaiah 11. John changes his Apocalyptic symbol, however, for Christ, and in verse 6, Christ is the Lamb that was slain. The horns probably denote power as they do in the book of Daniel. The seven eyes possibly means complete knowledge.

Christ has full or complete knowledge of everything. In Revelation 1:4, 3:1, and 4:5, John had mentioned seven spirits; and in 1:4, these seven spirits were related to the seven churches of Asia, but in 5:6, these spirits are called the seven Spirits of God. Possibly John is referring to the Holy Spirit, the Spirit of God working in and through the churches but also emanating from God's own self.

The Lamb, or Jesus, takes the scroll from the one on the throne, or God. Then, all the creatures and the elders worship the Lamb (similar to 4:9–10). They sing a new song. The new song (5:9–10) is that, because the Lamb was slain, he is therefore worthy to be worshiped and to receive great honor. Because he was slain, all nations, not just Jews, have been made a kingdom and priest to God. This idea that Christians are a part of the kingdom of God is basic New Testament thought

4 THE OPENING OF THE SCROLLS

and found in nearly every book. In Chapter 2 of Ephesians, Paul became very excited about the Gentiles or non-Jews all becoming "fellow citizens with God's people and members of God's household" (v 19). This was all brought about by the Lamb that was slain and causes all heaven, including millions of angels, to rejoice and give all honor and glory to the lamb. So chapter 5 ends with that beautiful doxology to the Lamb of God, who really did take away the sins of the world (see John 1:29).

4
THE OPENING OF THE SCROLLS

Revelation 6–7

As the lamb begins to open his seals in Revelation 6, the mystery of the content of the scroll becomes slowly visible. The action is rapid at the beginning, the first four seals taking only eight verses. The seventh seal, however, is not opened until chapter 8, and the last reference to the scroll is not found until chapter 10.

The reader is reminded that the Apocalyptist writes to his time. His message is to God's people suffering persecution or about to do so. Events are taking place right then during the lifetime of the author. If we want to know what is going on that causes the writing, it is necessary to know the approximate date of the writer. Since John mentions churches by name, he would have to be writing after those churches were established. Most possibly all of the churches were established by Paul or his associates (see Acts 19:10 and Colossians 1:5–8, 2:1–2, 4:13–17). Since Paul died in either AD 64 or 67 (Paul's date is determined by references outside the New Testament; these are mainly from church leaders known in history as Church Fathers), Revelation would have to have been written in the last quarter of the first century. (The church at Smyrna was not established until AD 64.) Since the churches had suffered some decay before the book of Revelation was written, the persecution was probably not that of Nero, which took place in AD 65. The major persecuting power during that period was the

Roman empire under the emperor Domitian. Revelation talks about people worshiping a beast. Most authorities believe that to be a reference to emperor worship. Although for many years, Roman emperors were to be objects of worship, few of them took it seriously. Domitian insisted upon being worshiped and expected to be called lord and god. There is ample evidence of serious Christian persecution during his reign. The reason, of course, was the conflict between the Christian worship of God and the emperor worship demanded by Domitian. Domitian's dates are AD 81–96, and most authorities believe that the Revelation of John was written near the end of that reign.

The Four Horsemen
Revelation 6:1–8

The curtain rises; the mystery of the sealed scroll is about to be revealed. The Lamb opens the seals, one by one. With a voice of thunder, one of the living creatures says, "Come," and out comes four horses one after the other: a white horse, a bright red horse, a black horse, and a pale horse. The rider on the first horse (white) had a bow, which symbolizes a foreign invasion (see Is 5:26ff and Jer 1:14). A crown was given him, and he went forth conquering and to conquer (Rev 6:1–2). The rider of the red horse was "given power to take peace from the earth and to make men slay each other," or conduct civil war (16:4). He was given a great sword (v 4). The rider of the black horse had a balance in his hand and a voice said, "A quart of wheat for a day's wages, and three quarts of barley for a day's wages, and do not damage the oil and the wine!" (v 6). The result of war without and within is famine.[1] The phrase "do not damage the oil or the wine" may have referred to a Domitian decree in AD 92 demanding that vineyards be destroyed and the land devoted to grain. The rider of the pale horse was named death,

---

1. Kiddle, *Revelation*, 115.

and Hades followed him (vv 7–8). They were given power over a fourth part of the earth.

What could all this mean? Most authorities believe that the first horse and rider represented an invasion by a foreign power. The second, or red, horse represented civil strife, since "men slay each other." The third, or black, horse represented famine, and the fourth or pale horse represented death, the usual results of war and famine.

What greater comfort could be given to suffering people than to learn that their persecutor is soon to pass from the scene. The Revelation of God through John was fulfilled by AD 500. The Roman Empire had invasion after invasion. They also suffered civil war and famine and finally suffered complete decline and death. The fall of the Roman Empire is usually dated about AD 500.

The Fifth and Sixth Seals
Revelation 6:9–17

But what of those who had already been killed, the martyrs who had not lived to see this judgment of God? The fifth seal (6:9–11) gives the living church encouragement by showing that the martyrs are under the altar, that is, in heaven. They were each given a white robe (see Daniel 12:10 where those who were faithful were in white) and told to rest awhile. Judgment would come upon the evil empire.

The sixth seal (Rev 6:12–17) shows more calamities, earthquakes, darkness, and stars falling from the sky. Just as Jesus associated the destruction of Jerusalem (AD 70) with the end of the world, so the revelator associates the final death of the Roman Empire with return of the Son of Man on clouds of glory (see the little Apocalypse for a similar description, Matthew 24:29; Luke 21:25 or Mark 13:24, where Jesus was talking about the destruction of Jerusalem, which did occur in AD 70, and the end of the world).

Perhaps it was necessary for the complete comfort of the suffering church to be reminded that evil will ultimately be destroyed and that God and good will live eternally. Evil will suffer both in this world and in the next. God and good will triumph both in this world and in the next. In other words, Christian, you can't lose. What hope and what joy! Even if you are misunderstood now, or even if killed for your faith, you are the winner. We need the book of Revelation even if we aren't expecting to be killed. We need it to remind us that unkindness, ill will toward others, harsh words toward friends and family, never pay off. In every sense, good conquers evil, a soft answer turns away wrath, and the only victory is love for one's enemies. If judgment is to be made, we are told to leave it to the wrath of God (Rom 12:19–20).

In John's generation, the earthquake and the cosmic disturbances could have meant the downfall of civilization, which is the prelude to the coming of the Son of Man with judgment and the end of the world.

The Triumph of the Martyrs
Revelation 7

The four winds were a well-known Apocalyptic symbol meaning judgment (see for example Daniel 7:2–3). The four corners of the earth, used often in ancient writing, was merely a way of saying that the calamities were universal. The destruction is not to come until the servants of God are sealed (Rev 7:3). The number 144,000 (vv 4–5) is not to be taken literally, anymore than the sealing in the forehead is to be taken literally. As seven was a sacred number, so also was twelve and ten, or multiples of these numbers. It probably means complete as the number seven. Christians were considered the true Israel, thus all tribes (vv 5–9) are used as symbols of every single Christian being sealed by God. The seal is not described. Perhaps what John really meant was "we are sealed with the Holy Spirit" (see

4 THE OPENING OF THE SCROLLS

Ephesians 1:13–14). The major point is that God is aware of every one of his children and takes care of them. That is really the major point of these symbols.

John then sees a whole multitude in white robes from every nation under heaven, carrying palm branches and singing praises to God and to the Lamb. All in heaven fall down before the throne and worship God. All of this great multitude are those who have come through the Great Tribulation (persecution).

Perhaps one of the most comforting passages in all of Scripture, at least comforting to those who have suffered, is found in chapter 7:15–17.

> He who sits on the throne will spread his tent over them. Never again will they hunger; never again will they thirst. The sun will not beat upon them, nor any scorching heat. For the Lamb at the center of the throne will be their shepherd; he will lead them to springs of living water. And God will wipe away every tear from their eyes.

5
THE WOES OF THE SEVEN TRUMPETS

Revelation 8–11

The Seventh Seal
Revelation 8

When the seventh seal is opened there is silence in heaven for half an hour. This probably means only that there is a pause before the next series of calamities are given.

John sees the seven angels who stand before God. Each is given a trumpet. Before the trumpets are blown, another scene is portrayed. Another angel appears with incense representing the prayers of the saints. After this, the angel took the censer, filled it with fire, and cast it to the earth. The events following are similar to those recorded in 5:8. (Remember John's method of recapitulation that was defined in chapter 3. For more information on recapitulation, see Appendix B.)

The seven angels then made ready to blow their trumpets (v 6). The calamities of the seven trumpets were as follows: The first trumpet was followed by fire and hail (v 7); the second trumpet, a roaring volcano (vv 8–9); the third, burning meteorites (8:10–11); the fourth, an eclipse of the sun, moon, and stars, bringing darkness (v 12). The eagle crying, "Woe, woe, woe," may have symbolized the Roman Empire, since this was their major ensign (v 13).

Considerable detail is given of the calamities following the blowing of the fifth trumpet (9:1–11). Another star, probably symbolizing an angel, falls from heaven. The angel is given the key to the bottomless pit. Locusts come from the pit, peculiar creatures with the power of scorpions, shaped like horses for battle but with faces like men and crowns on their head.

The description of the invading army (vv 13–21) is horrible, and John probably wanted it to be so. The woes of the seven trumpets depict calamity and destruction as had the symbols of the events in chapters 5 and 6. John is using the principle of recapitulation (defined in Appendix B). John means to repeat himself, for he is in dead earnest and wants the church to get the message clearly, so he repeats. To keep from being boring, he changes his symbols after each series. His first description of the woes to come is very reserved. It becomes more and more descriptive and terrible as he progresses. Each series seems to build upon the former series, but each succeeding series gives greater detail. Each set of symbols tells the same general story: punishment of the evil empire, the security of the people of God, and the power and majesty of the One who is on the throne and the Lamb whose death brought salvation.

The Two Witnesses
Revelation 11

The woes are interrupted by the appearance of a strong angel with a scroll that John is asked to eat. It will seem sweet because it is the destiny God has planned, but it will be bitter in his stomach. As with Ezekiel (3:1, 14) there was much bitterness in proclaiming a message of doom. This comforting section continues in chapter 11 with some disturbing symbols of warning to the church. Christians are to be measured to determine if they are true or false. Most authorities believe the two witnesses were Moses and Elijah (Rev 11:3–14). The description certainly points that way. The phrase "shut up the sky so that it will not

5 THE WOES OF THE SEVEN TRUMPETS

rain during the time they are prophesying" is descriptive of Elijah. The "power to turn the waters into blood and to strike the earth with every kind of plague" illustrates the life of Moses and the plagues in Egypt. Probably evil men did rejoice at the death of these two great men (v 10). These two also appeared with Jesus at the transfiguration and were representative of the Jewish religious system, its law, and its prophets. So probably, John means these two to be representative of Jewish religion in his vision. The statement of the resurrection of these two great men would give comfort to the suffering church.

The Problem of Numbers

There has been much speculation about the numbers mentioned in 11:2–3 (42 months or 1,260 days). Some people try to interpret these as 1,260 years and see their own denomination arising at the end of that time. Unfortunately, they often see other religious groups becoming the beast that is described in the last part of Revelation. This is to completely misunderstand Apocalyptic writing. The writer did not mean to be taken literally. He did not expect us to see literal numbers. He wrote in symbols because he had to do so to comfort the church during its trial. If he had written plainly, the message would never have reached the church. The persecutors would have destroyed it. One must be consistent also and not have one part of the book symbolic and the rest literal. One must try to stand where the writer stood, understand the situation of his day. The comfort he gave to the church at that time is always timely. It is always true and meets the need of humankind in every age. The truth is that God is great. God's kingdom will overcome evil. God's people will triumph. God cares about every single one of his people. God will triumph; evil will be destroyed ultimately. These are words of comfort to God's people in every age and to us individually in our small and great trials.

Conclusion to the Series
Revelation 11:15–19

As in other series of symbols, John passes from the earthly to the heavenly scene so that the believer can see the result of his hope. The great voices in heaven mark the climax of John's vision. We hear again the beautiful words that form the basis of the Hallelujah chorus of the musical production *The Messiah*: "The kingdom of the world has become the kingdom of our Lord and of his Christ, and he will reign for ever and ever" (v 15). Thus closes the first half of John's vision, a fitting pause before his next series of woes.

6
THE WOMAN, THE DRAGON, AND THE BEAST

Revelation 12–14

The Women and the Beast
Revelation 12

With chapter 12 John begins a whole new series of visions, more elaborate and more interesting than earlier ones. He had talked about seven seals and then about seven trumpets. His major message will be repeated but with a somewhat different emphasis.

Notice that several events in the Apocalypse take place in "heaven." This word really means sky. John means that the events are very easy to see. It would be like our saying, "I could see it as plain as day."

To most people, the symbol of the woman means the church. The woman is about to bear a child. It is believed that the child symbolizes the new converts. Her pain shows the sorrow of the church for sinful humanity whom she wants born into the kingdom of God (see Gal 4:26–27). Her very agony of soul brings children into the kingdom. John probably uses the phrase "male child" deliberately. Male children were very precious in the Middle East. John also may want a contrast between the strong and pure church (male child) and the evil harlot daughters mentioned in chapter 17.

Notice the description of the woman clothed with the sun and the moon under her feet and crowned with twelve stars (v 1). This probably symbolized her beauty and heavenly power. This is the church, the beautiful church with power from heaven.

The red dragon (v 3) is identified with the devil and Satan (v 9).[1] The early church realized that the battle was not "against flesh and blood, but against the rulers, against the authorities, against the powers of this dark world" (Eph 6:12). John is emphasizing in this section the supernatural evil forces back of the persecution. Times have not changed in the spirit world. The forces of evil are still around. Satan did not give up his power when the scientific age was born. Christians always need to be alert and trusting in God who is their strength. The seven heads, ten horns, and seven crowns illustrate the earthly powers controlled by the dragon (Satan). Notice how the dragon waits to devour the child (new Christians) as soon as he is born. The child is caught up to God. John may be referring to the martyrs.

The persecuted church flees to the wilderness, where she is nourished by God for 1,260 days. The meaning? Our symbols today would be "the church went underground and fed her soul on the Word of God and was comforted by God's Spirit."

The 1,260 days are repeated several times in the book. Sometimes John refers to them as forty-two months. This probably means a long time. It would probably be necessary for John to remind the church that she must brace herself for a long period of suffering. They will not immediately see God's judgment on their persecutors. Judgment will come, however, as John shows in the following verses (vv 7–9). As in Daniel (see Daniel 10:13, 21; 12:1), the angel Michael and his angels fight against the dragon. His being cast out of heaven possibly means that Satan can never destroy the church. Isn't this what Jesus said in Matthew 16, "I will build my church, and the gates

---

1. See Appendix C.

of Hades will not prevail against it" (NRSV)? Good overcomes evil. God is superior to Satan. The church will stand forever.

When the New Testament speaks of the church, it does not mean a building or even an institution. The word means those who are called out by God to be his people. Every true Christian is a part of the church. Possibly in every age, Christians need to be reminded that even the gates of hell cannot win against them.

The victory over the dragon (Satan) is followed by singing in heaven (vv 10–12). The song tells how the dragon was conquered: They overcame "by the blood of the Lamb and by the word of their testimony; they did not love their lives so much as to shrink from death" (v 11). The church is purified and grows through persecution. Persecution is the seed of the church.

But the dragon (Satan) wasn't finished. Angered because of his defeat, he persecutes the woman (church) again. She is rescued by an eagle and is nourished in the wilderness.

Some theories of interpretation make "the wilderness" the dark ages, literalizing the 1,260 days as years. This, of course, is contrary to Apocalyptic thought and method. It is difficult to give exact dates for the Dark or Middle Ages. Probable dates are roughly from the fall of Rome, AD 500, to the Protestant Reformation and the Renaissance, or about the sixteenth century.

It would be very comfortable to believe that the Dark Ages of ignorance and blindness to spiritual truth and freedom is in the past. The fact is that blindness to God's truth is a type of darkness. The church is always in danger from prejudice and religious bigotry. Only the sincere study of God's Word and constant dependence upon the leading of the Spirit can protect us from our worse selves, which Paul calls the flesh (see Romans, chapter 8).

The dragon (Satan) was overcome "by the blood of the Lamb and by the word of their [Christian] testimony." Things still operate very much the same way today. A testimony is not just words said in prayer meeting. It is mainly life lived under fire in offices, shops, schools, and places of amusement. As John said, "Now have come the salvation and the power and the kingdom of our God, and the authority of his Christ. For the accuser of our brothers, who accuses them before our God day and night, has been hurled down" (Rev 12:10). Satan is thrown down any time even the simplest Christian overcomes the evil of temptation, hypocrisy, and the moral compromise so characteristic of modern society.

The river coming out of the dragon's mouth may merely mean that the flood tides of evil can never destroy the Church. Isaiah (43:2–3) says it beautifully:

> When you pass through the waters, I will be with you; and when you pass through the rivers, they will not sweep over you. When you walk through the fire, you will not be burned; the flames will not set you ablaze. For I am the Lord, your God.

The beautiful picture of the church in chapter 12 (a woman clothed with the sun and the moon under her feet) shows the church in agony for the child about to be born (v 2). Sorrow among Christians for sinful humanity seems to be a lost art. Perhaps we are not enough aware of the real issues. Most moderns do not really believe that there is a spiritual warfare going on, that is, evil forces attempting to destroy God's children. Is evil so much a part of our culture that we do not even recognize it? Is it possible that we are so far from God that we are confused about priorities? God is for real. God's goodness is for real. His judgment is for real, and the devil is for real. Erase any one of these and life is lopsided. There is nothing left but perishable things. Jesus warned us about this: "Do not work for food that spoils, but for food that endures to eternal life" (John 6:27).

Which of these gets the major part of our time, our energy, our money, and our thoughts: The food that perishes or that which endures to eternal life?

The Beast
Revelation 13:1-10

Another terrible animal comes on the scene as this series builds to a climax. Note how much more vivid is the description of the beast than that of the dragon. Perhaps that is because the beast is more visible. The dragon was the supernatural power of evil or Satan. The dragon gave his power to the beast (13:4), so we know the beast is evil. Men worshiped the dragon (v 4) and they worshiped the beast. John is contrasting two powers or two kingdoms: The power of God versus the power of Satan, which is expressed by Christian worship versus the worship of the beast. The beast is therefore visible just as Christians are visible. But who is the beast? Note his description in verses 5-8: He blasphemes God and heaven. He makes war on the saints and conquerors them. He has authority over every tribe and tongue. All who dwell on the earth worship him except those whose names are in the Book of Life. The only person in the first century who completely meets this description was the emperor Domitian. The emperor Nero had also persecuted the Christians, but it was not because of their failure to worship the emperor.

The beast is sometimes believed to be the Pope in Rome, or to have been Hitler or the Communists. These views have to be rejected. The Apocalyptist always speaks to the people of his time. John is talking about the danger happening right then. Persecution had already started. John himself was sharing the "Great Tribulation." He "was on the island of Patmos because of the word of God and the testimony of Jesus" (Rev 1:9). The faithful witness Antipas had already been killed (2:13). More persecution was to come. It would last a long time (the symbol of forty-two months). Christians were to be patient and not retaliate: If anyone is to be taken captive, to captivity he goes; if anyone slays with the sword, with the sword must he be slain (13:9).

The idea of nonretaliation was and is basic Christian doctrine. You will remember that Jesus said in the Sermon on the Mount that we are to love our enemies and we are to turn the other cheek (Matt 5; Luke 6). Paul had said, "Do not take revenge" (Rom 12:19).

In Revelation 13:3, John speaks of the beast having a mortal wound that was healed. Most authorities believe that this was a reference to the reign of Nero. When Nero died, many people believed that the Roman Empire would fall (had a mortal wound), but the empire revived and became stronger than ever (the wound healed). The emperor Domitian is "the second Nero."[2] The healing of the wound is a symbol "indicating an emperor who was a persecutor as Nero was."[3] It is the spirit of Nero revived, for the same evil forces that drove Nero to kill hundreds of Christians including Peter and Paul, has driven Domitian to kill innocent people. Morris reminds us that the power of evil may seem to be defeated but never is. It arises again and again.

Another Beast
Revelation 13:11–18

The second beast has no crowns, and so he does not represent civil authority. Notice that "he exercised all the authority of the first beast...and made the earth and its inhabitants worship the first beast" (v 12). This second beast is more clearly identified by John in Revelation 16:13, 19:20, and 20:10, where the beast is called the false prophet.

---

2. Linn, *Hebrew to Revelation*, 122.
3. Rist, "Revelation," 461.

6 THE WOMAN, THE DRAGON, AND THE BEAST

The "causing fire to come down from heaven" is a reference to works of magic often performed by pagans of that time. The signs were done to deceive people and cause them to worship the beast (vv 13–14). Jesus had warned his disciples that false prophets would "appear and perform great signs and miracles to deceive even the elect—if that were possible" (Matt 24:24).

The number 666 probably does not mean to refer to any person in our time. The number is probably completely symbolic as other numbers in the book of Revelation are. The number seven was a sacred number, usually meaning completeness. Six is the number under seven, symbolizing incompleteness and nonperfection. John wanted to be certain that the Christians got the message, so he repeated it three times, thus 6, 6, 6, or 666. It is something like your mother said to you when you were about to do something wrong, "No, no, no," each "no" getting louder than the former one. Perhaps the number refers to "every man." As someone has said, "Unregenerate man always falls short."[4] (Morris 174).

Revelation 13:12 says that this beast exercises all the authority of the first beast and makes the inhabitants worship the first beast. This sounds very much like the priests of the imperial cult, who were not rulers, thus no crowns, but enforced the worship of the emperor (the beast). Failure to give pledges of loyalty to the emperor resulted in economic boycotts and business failures. The Christians were threatened at every point, both socially and economically.

History is replete with illustrations of Rome's persecution of the Christians. Both Peter and Paul apparently died during the horrible persecution by Nero (AD 64). Tacitus, a Roman historian, tells how Christians suffered at that time. Some were crucified, some were sewn up in the skins of animals and hunted down by dogs, some were covered with pitch and set alight to serve as living torches when darkness fell. Apparently all of this served as entertainment for Nero, who outwardly

---

4. Morris, *Revelation of St. John*, 174.

gave the excuse that Christians had set fire to the city of Rome. Although these events preceded the writing of the book of Revelation, the scene is probably in the memory of the writer and many of his readers.

By the time of Domitian (AD 81–96), Christians were considered as enemies of the state, mainly because of their refusal to worship the Roman gods. There is very little Roman data for the persecution under Domitian. The fact that John had to write his book in symbols shows that the persecution was very severe. John himself was suffering banishment because of that persecution, and at least one Christian had already been killed as John began to write (Rev 2:13). Domitian insisted upon being worshiped, and Christians could not possibly go along with that. The result was persecution of the Christians.

In the book of Revelation, John warns that more severe trials are to follow. Later history has proved the validity of those predictions. The Roman Empire persecuted the church until the beginning of the fourth century. There is more information from Roman sources regarding persecution at the time of the emperor Trajan because of various letters written at the time that have come down to us. The issue was secret societies, which Emperor Trajan had banned. Christianity was considered a secret society and Christians were apparently considered as enemies of the state.[5] Some Christians were true to their convictions, and many were executed because of it. Other Christians apparently gave in to the political pressure, which caused much confusion in the churches. John had warned about that also. The Christian leader Ignatius died during that persecution, as did Symenon, the successor to James, the Lord's brother.

Trajan's successors, the emperors Hadrian and Antonius Pius followed the same general policy set by Trajan. Persecution became more intense with Marchus Aurelius. By

---

5. For further information, see F. F. Bruce, *New Testament History* (New York: Doubleday, 1969) 424ff.

6 THE WOMAN, THE DRAGON, AND THE BEAST

AD 140, Christians were accused of (a) cannibalism, because of a misunderstanding of the Lord's Supper; (b) licentiousness, because it was celebrated at night; (c) atheism, for refusal to worship the old gods; and (d) anarchy, because of opposition to emperor worship. By AD 250, persecution of the Christians had become general throughout the empire.

During the one thousandth anniversary of the founding of Rome, there were mob attacks on Christians. Many Christians were tortured, some died, and some gave up their faith to avoid trouble. Thus, the persecution did last a long time as John had said. That Christians were tortured beyond description is verified by Eusebius, who says that

> The Christians in Thebius were scraped over the entire body with shells until they died...They were bound to heavy branches of trees. The stoutest branches were brought together with machines, the limbs of the martyrs were bound to them. The branches were then allowed to resume their natural position, instantly tearing asunder the bodies of those who were bound. This horrible death was carried on by the Roman emperors. Christians were decapitated, tortured by fire, while watching their brethren die other Christians rushed to the judgment seat confessing themselves Christians, indifferent to the torture."[6]

Linn says, "further description is too revolting to be given here." John not only experienced the early days of this persecution but saw by divine revelation what the future held for Christians under the Roman Empire with its horrible imperial cult (the beast arising out of the earth). John was very

---

6. Eusebius, *History of the Christian Church*, quoted in Linn, *Hebrews to Revelation*, 123–25.

serious about the message. Christians needed to know what was to come and understand that the kingdom of God would ultimately triumph over this horrible kingdom of evil.

A Message of Hope
Revelation 14

John must have been a good preacher. Each time he shows the evil powers and horrible conditions that the Christians are experiencing, he follows with a description of their hope. He shows God on his throne or the angels praising God or the Christ who was slain. He always ends with a triumphant statement of God's conquest over evil. This series is no exception. John wants the church to really get the message of hope, so he repeats that message three times under different symbols.

The first symbol is the Lamb (Christ) standing on Mount Zion. How marvelous for the suffering church to get this message of cheer. No lesser being than Christ himself is shown to them. The church (the 144,000) is around the Lamb singing a new song, the song of redemption. I can just imagine the Christian on earth saying, "It was all worth it after all."

The second symbol shows another angel (vv 6–7), who takes a message to the Christians on earth. The message is to "fear God and give him glory, because the hour of his judgment has come." In other words, don't give in, Christians, to the evil imperial cult. It will one day be judged and destroyed.

The third symbol is another angel, who says, "Fallen! Fallen is Babylon the Great" (v 8). Babylon was the ancient symbol for Rome (see 1 Peter 5:13). Rome is going to fall because she "made all the nations drink the maddening wine of her adulteries." The Roman Empire in the first century did encompass all nations around the Mediterranean Seas, so the phrase "all the nations" was often used as the description of the empire.

6 THE WOMAN, THE DRAGON, AND THE BEAST

The third angel gives a warning to the Christians that "if anyone worships the beast…he, too, will drink of the wine of God's fury… This calls for patient endurance on the part of the saints" (vv 9–12). John is a genius, or rather he is depending upon genius, which is the revelation of God. He follows this severe warning with the comforting voice of the Lord: "Blessed are the dead who die in the Lord" (v 13).

Judgment of the wickedness of the earth is portrayed in the rest of chapter 14 by the Son of man and angels with sharp sickles. The judgment is symbolized by a great winepress with blood flowing from it for two hundred miles.

7
THE SEVEN BOWLS

Revelation 15–16

The Seven Angels
Revelation 15

The events in chapters 15 and 16 are similar to those of chapters 8 and 9. The symbols change. Chapter 8 spoke of seven angels with seven trumpets. Chapter 15 speaks of seven angels with seven bowls. In both series, a picture of divinity and of Christians appears before the judgment is given. The Lamb appears in chapter 8, and a sea of glass, probably a synonym of God, is shown in chapter 15. The prayers precede the judgment in chapter 8. A song of praise to God precedes the plagues in chapter 15. John often repeats himself in the Apocalypse. Symbol after symbol tells the same story. You wonder why. Probably the same reason that basic rules were often repeated to you when you were at home with your parents.

Think how often the preacher has to tell the congregation to give, or how often he or she tells the sinners to repent. John doesn't run out of symbols with which to repeat his message. There was apparently a very extensive Apocalyptic vocabulary among his listeners. The message of the terror is so serious that it bears repeating many times.

The bowls are to be poured out on the earth very much like the golden censer full of fire was poured out in chapter 8 (vv 3–5).

The mention of prayer (chapter 8) and praise (chapter 15) is probably not accidental. There is no better way of meeting adversity, temptation, or fear, or any other trouble than by prayer and praise. The message John gives was certainly meant to meet the needs of the Christians of his day, but the basic principles in this book are timeless. Do we meet our problems by first praying and praising God? Or do we try everything else first and turn to God only as a last resort when things are hopeless.

The Bowls Poured Out Upon the Earth
Revelation 16

One after another, the seven bowls were poured out upon the earth: sores, water turned to blood, burning heat, darkness, foul spirits like frogs, and a great earthquake. Some of these were similar to the plagues on Egypt in the book of Exodus. Since John is speaking figuratively, the bowls could be civil war, strife, or invasion, as well as natural catastrophes. The reference to "kings of the east" (v 12) possibly implies an invasion. The exact meaning of the symbols is not important. The fact is that the Roman Empire is either going to fall or be destroyed because of its evil treatment of the Christians.

There has been too much made of the word *Armageddon* (v 16). John only mentions it one time. Some people connect it with Revelation 20:8 and make the two scriptures apply to the same event to a great battle at the time of the millennial reign of Christ on earth. "Gog and Magog" (Rev 20:8) was based on Ezekiel 38–39, which, according to scholars, was often used by the Jews in reference to the Messianic Kingdom. Both scriptures do speak of a battle, but since John is using symbolic language, it is probably not a literal, physical battle that is meant. One must remember John's basic message that related to the Roman Empire.

7 THE SEVEN BOWLS

It is not at all certain what Armageddon meant. Some think it meant the city of Megiddo from Zechariah 12:11. Others think it meant Mount Carmel, while others believe Jerusalem is meant. It probably is not important what the symbol meant. What is important is John's basic message. The Roman Empire is going to be destroyed. To say this without the Romans "catching on," John used this term *Armageddon*. Megiddo would be a good guess because the Jews suffered some very serious defeats there. Two of their kings were killed at Megiddo. Linn says that John's statement about Armageddon would be like saying, "He met his Waterloo."[1]

---

1. Linn, *Hebrews to Revelation*, 12

8
JUDGMENT ON THE EMPIRE

Revelation 17–18

The Harlot
Revelation 17

The harlot is probably a symbol for Roman civilization. The "many waters" would then refer to the Mediterranean Sea. Roman civilization encompassed all the areas around the Mediterranean Sea. The sea is further explained in verse 15 as peoples and nations.

The angel takes John to the desert. The desert, or wilderness as it is usually called, had been glorified by some Jewish thinkers, particularly the prophets (note Hosea 13:5; Jeremiah 2:2; 3 1:2). The usual meaning is the time when God led the children of Israel through the wilderness by the hand of Moses, who had saved them from Egyptian slavery. It was in the desert or wilderness that Moses was called by God to lead the people. It was in the wilderness that the miracles of manna and of water were performed. It was in the wilderness that people first accepted God and the laws were given to them from Mount Sinai. Perhaps John used it here to show that in the wilderness he is given true perspective about the affairs of life. Perhaps the wilderness did for John what our "quiet time" does for us. Years before, both Jesus and the apostle Paul had gone into the wilderness or desert to think and to meditate about God or to be tested for future work for God.

From this place, the wilderness, John sees the true meaning of Roman civilization. The woman sits on a scarlet beast covered with blasphemous titles. The seven heads and ten horns show the beast's identity, the same as the one mentioned in chapter 13, or the Roman rulers.

Harlotry was often used to describe idol worship (note, for example, Hosea 2:5, 3:3, 4:15; Nahum 3:4; and Is 23:15–16). Her immoral daughters may mean that she was the leader and promoted other pagan gods and goddesses. This description aptly fits Roman civilization.

To try to identify the seven kings as the emperors of Rome is probably as fruitless as looking for the Holy Grail. The number seven means complete as it does in the rest of the Apocalypse. John probably means all the emperors of Rome. This is a position taken by Kiddle.

The woman sitting on the beast possibly symbolizes the force or the power of the beast or of the Roman emperors that make the woman or Roman civilization possible.

The major theme is that Roman civilization will fall because the woman or civilization has failed to worship God; she has propagated idol worship and was "drunk with the blood of the saints, the blood of those who bore testimony to Jesus" (v 6). This was her major sin.

The beast who carried the woman will be conquered by the Lamb (v 14), another major idea in the Apocalypse.

The Fall of Babylon
Revelation 18

An angel appears (18:2) calling, "Fallen! Fallen is Babylon the Great." The literal city of Babylon was the capital of the Babylonian Empire. It was the empire that had conquered the Jews in 587 BC, burning their city and destroying their temple. It was a large empire, for Babylon had conquered many nations. At that time, many people believed that wars were won by the strongest god. Many Jews, therefore, began to worship the Babylonian god, Marduk. The conquest and the resulting apostasy by many Jews led the prophets to denounce Babylon. Both Isaiah (21) and Jeremiah (50) give poems about the final judgment of the ancient city of Babylon.

John's description of the fall of Rome (that is, Babylon) are very similar to that of Jeremiah 50 concerning the ancient city of Babylon. That Babylon was the name given for Rome was mentioned in Revelation 14. It is not only given in 1 Peter, but it was also given by a number of Jewish writers in the period between the writing of the Old and New Testaments.

The merchants weep when Rome falls (vv 11–19) because they will lose business. The kings (vv 9–10) of the earth weep possibly because they fear they will be next. The seamen and merchants weep because their economic security is also involved with Rome. Rome was a very wealthy city. It was the capital of a great empire and thus, made money off of all those under its dominion.

As most great cities, it was full of sin. Its greatest evil was its emperor worship and the resulting persecutions of the Christians. Because of this, it will fall. By divine revelation, John sees the fall (vv 21–24). He shows its desolation with no inhabitants, no business, nothing happening in the city.

The phrase "come out of her, my people" (v 4) is directed at the church. Come out of her is probably a call to refrain from any kind of association with the imperial cult. There were undoubtedly Christians who thought burning incense to the emperor was a small thing, that it was not important, that it was not acceptance of the imperial cult. It is possibly that, this is the kind of compromise against which John is warning the church. If the churches of Asia, which we considered all of the churches, were any indication of the church's life in the first century, a warning to God's people was certainly needed. It is probably always needed. Though many things seem so simple and harmless, very soon the church ceases to be the church.

A COMMONSENSE APPROACH TO...REVELATION

In John's day as well as in our own, we need to fear moral compromise and earthly distractions. How important John's message is for our time.

9
THE TRIUMPH OF CHRIST

Revelation 19:1–22:5

The Hallelujahs
Revelation 19:1–10

In the first ten verses occur what is called the four hallelujahs. Time after time in the Apocalypse, John follows words of judgment with words of cheer and hope, with pictures of God, the Lamb, or the songs of angels. Each scene of judgment was more elaborate than the former one, and each song of triumphant more impressive than that which had gone before.

In this section, there are four hallelujahs. The word in Hebrew means "Praise ye the Lord." It is not used elsewhere in the New Testament and occurs most often in the book of Psalms. The first two hallelujahs in the Apocalypse celebrate the destruction of the evil woman (vv 1–3). The idea of choruses in heaven singing and rejoicing at destruction at all is very difficult for many moderns to accept. We need to remember that the woman in the Apocalypse is not a literal woman but Roman civilization. It is the principle of evil that is being destroyed and good people should rejoice at that.

Praise is given to God in all four hallelujahs. The fourth hallelujah (vv 6–8) celebrates the marriage of the Lamb. This should be a familiar figure. In both Old Testament and New, the people of God are said to be God's wife (see Hosea 2:19–20; Is 54:5–6; Ezekiel 16:6–14), or the bride of Christ. For

Jesus as the bridegroom see Matthew 25:1–13; Mark 2:19–20. And for the church as the bride, see Ephesians 5:22–23. John is probably using the same symbolism here. The bride is the church who has kept herself pure and spotless for her husband (Rev 19:8; compare with 2 Corinthians 11:2 and Ephesians 5:27).

Jesus compared his return to a marriage feast Matthew 22:1–14; 25:1–13, and Luke 12:35–38). In each of the above parables, the Christian is to be ready, to be awake. He is reminded that no one knows the hour when the Son of man comes. He is to watch and to be ready.

In chapter 19 of the Apocalypse, John sees the marriage feast. The Bride is ready, clothed in "fine linen, bright and clean" (v 8). The benediction, "Blessed are those who are invited to the wedding supper of the Lamb," causes the angel to bid John write, "These are the true words of God" (v 9). This was all too much for John. He fell to the ground in front of the angel. The angel forbids John to worship him in this way, for the angel is only a fellow servant. John is told to worship God (v 10).

The phrase "the testimony of Jesus is the spirit of prophecy" is a reminder that while on the island of Patmos, John was called to write what he saw (note 1:10–11). This gives the writing of the entire book the necessary authority. John's revelations are not wild dreams. They are God's truth for God's children, in a time of serious and eternal trial and conflict.

Verses 11–16 show the appearance of the Lord. The most essential belief in all of Christianity is the belief that Jesus Christ is the Son of God, the Word made flesh, King of Kings and Lord of Lords. Here he is shown on a white horse; he is called faithful and true. The armies of heaven follow him. The suffering Christian who holds to his faith and refuses to indulge in anything related to the imperial cult is not alone. All the armies of heaven are back of him. It is not a literal army or a literal battle. It is the promise of the presence of the Lord himself standing beside the Christian, breathing strength into him, giving freely of his wisdom and all the graces of his Spirit.

By divine revelation John saw again and again the bare truth. He saw the battle joined and knew how it would end. With the imperial cult having a stranglehold on society and politics, there seemed no hope for the Christians of the time. John comes with hope. Evil will be destroyed. The boast and the false prophet will be cast into the lake of fire. All the armies of the world fought against the One on the white horse and lost. This was Christ triumphant. If you are on his side, you can never lose. If you are killed, you still win because you go to be with him. In a sense, you never die.

There is a subtle battle going on all of the time in our world, year after year, decade after decade. It is the battle for people's minds and souls. The enemy never sleeps. He is of another world but breaks constantly into this one. He is seeking whom he may devour (1 Pet 5:8). This is very clear in the scriptures and in human experience. To act as though this were not true is to be very blind or very ignorant or both. The bright person, the intelligent person is that one who has saturated his or her mind with the great promises of God and lives them out in society day by day. No matter how difficult the task or impossible the environment, the One on the white horse is leading his army against the fiery darts of the Devil (Eph 6:16). "If God is for us, who can be against us?... Who shall separate us from the love of Christ? Shall trouble or hardship or persecution or famine or nakedness or danger or sword?...No, in all these things we are more than conquerors through him who loved us" (Rom 8:31, 35, 37). With promises like these, how can we lose hope?

The Thousand Years
Revelation 20

Chapter 20 is very controversial. It has probably caused more excitement and generated more theological heat than any other chapter in the Bible. Although there are variations of theories, the entire debate can possibly be placed under two headings: (1) The Premillennial View and, (2) The Non-millennial View. It will be necessary to look at both views in some detail.

Premillennial Theory

Generally speaking, the premillennial view is as follows:

1. When Christ comes again, he will set up his kingdom.
2. Satan will be bound for a thousand years.
3. The martyrs who have died will be resurrected and reign with Christ. That is the first resurrection.
4. During the thousand years, the government of Christ will be set up in Jerusalem from which the rest of the world is ruled.
5. This will be a time of peace because Satan is bound.
6. At the end of the thousand years, Satan is loosed and he deceives the nations, who are numerous as the sands of the sea.
7. The nations gather for battle against the camp of the saints (apparently in Jerusalem).
8. The battle is won by the saints because fire from heaven consumes the nations.
9. The devil is cast in the lake of fire.
10. Then comes the second resurrection. All the dead are raised and appear before the judgment.
11. Those whose names are not in the Book of Life are cast into the lake of fire. Many premillenialists use Isaiah 11:6–9 as a prophecy of the millennial reign: "The wolf will live with the lamb...the calf and the lion and the yearling together."

9 THE TRIUMPH OF CHRIST

Nonmillennial View

(The postmillennial view is very like the nonmillennial position.)
1. Christ's kingdom is not a literal kingdom. It was set up when he came to earth to die for our sins.
2. The binding of Satan took place when Jesus came into the world the first time and continues until he will come again.
3. The first resurrection is spiritual and refers to the conversion experience where the Christian is raised from death to life.
4. The word Jerusalem is spiritual, referring to the Christians or the church.
5. The thousand years is symbolic, meaning a long time.
6. The battles mentioned in Revelation are symbolic, meaning spiritual battles between good and evil or the Christian versus Satan.
7. There are not two physical resurrections a thousand years apart. All are resurrected at the same time—good and evil.

Which of these positions is the right one? How does one evaluate the theories? One's interpretation of any biblical truth should agree with the whole tenor (general meaning or aim) of Scripture. It should not contradict the major concepts in other parts of the Bible. This is particularly necessary when interpreting a symbolic book like the Apocalypse. In fact, it is best not to base any theory solely on a symbolic book. One can make the symbols mean anything one chooses. This is often done.

The first point in the above theories related to Christ's kingdom. Jesus said his kingdom was not of this world. He said if it were, his servants would fight (John 18:36). He told his disciples again and again not to be looking for the kingdom, because he said, "The kingdom of God does not come with your careful observation, nor will people say, 'Here it is,' or 'There it is,' because the kingdom of God is within you" (Luke 17:20–21). The kingdom came on the scene when Jesus began to preach. Jesus said, "If I drive out demons by the Spirit of God, then the kingdom of God has come upon you" (Matt 12:28). He had just finished casting out demons; in fact, this was the cause of the discussion. During Jesus' ministry, the kingdom was present, for he told the Jewish leaders that "the tax collectors and the prostitutes are entering the kingdom of God ahead of you" (Matt 21:31). Apparently, Jesus brought the kingdom when he himself first came into the world.

What about the binding of Satan (Rev 20:2)? Jesus implies that Satan was bound during his ministry. When Jesus was criticized for casting out demons, he said, "How can anyone enter a strong man's house and carry off his possessions unless he first ties up the strong man?" (Matt 12:29). Paul says that Christ through his death, "having disarmed the powers and authorities, he made a public spectacle of them" (Col 2:15). Paul believed that when God raised Christ from the dead, he "seated him at his right hand in the heavenly realms, far above all rule and authority, power and dominion" (Eph 1:20–21). Just before the cross event, Jesus said, "Now is the time for judgment on this world; now the prince of this world will be driven out" (John 12:31).

The idea that we are living in a period of time when Satan is bound seems contrary to common sense and to what we see on television and read in our daily newspapers. Crime and evil seem to be in the ascendancy. If we are going to keep the Apocalypse a symbolic book, we had better spiritualize the binding of Satan. If you are a child of God, Satan is bound for you and will remain so as long as, or to the degree that, you trust in the Lamb who was slain for you. That binding took place nearly two thousand years ago but is only a reality for you when you accept the Lord as your personal Savior. To make it

9 THE TRIUMPH OF CHRIST

universal and apply to the entire world is to miss the message Jesus came to give.

According to the New Testament, the first resurrection is salvation from sin. Several scriptures teach this. For example, John 5:24, 28–29 says, "Whoever hears my word and believes him who sent me has eternal life...has crossed over from death to life...a time is coming when all who are in their graves will hear his voice and come out—those who have done good will rise to live, and those who have done evil will rise to be condemned." There is implied here two resurrections: one spiritual, he who hears my word has eternal life or has passed from death unto life; and the other, physical, the day is coming when all who are in the tombs will hear my voice. Christian baptism was early interpreted as death, burial, and resurrection: "Wake up, O sleeper, rise from the dead, and Christ will shine on you" (Eph 5:14; see also Colossians 2:12–13). This is a clear indication that the first resurrection was spiritual.

The battles in Revelation are undoubtedly spiritual, also. It would be difficult to imagine Christ taking up a sword. It is contrary to his teachings and to the life he lived. When his followers wanted to defend him at the time of his arrest, Jesus said, "All who draw the sword will die by the sword" (Matt 26:52). He both taught and lived nonretaliation. Even in the book of Revelation, the suffering Christians who were being killed for their faith were to be patient: "If anyone is to go into captivity, into captivity he will go. If anyone is to be killed with the sword, with the sword he will be killed" (Rev 13:10). We are taught to love our enemies, to turn the other cheek. We are to follow the example of Jesus, who "suffered for you, leaving you an example, that you should follow in his steps. 'He committed no sin, and no deceit was found in his mouth.' When they hurled their insults at him, he did not retaliate; when he suffered, he made no threats" (1 Pet 2:21–23).

Perhaps something should be said about Gog and Magog, which have caused a great deal of speculation, particularly in our time. The terms *Gog* and *Magog* come from Ezekiel chapters 38 and 39. In an Apocalyptic vision, Ezekiel speaks of Gog, prince of Magog, and all his hordes as the people from the north who are about to fight against Jerusalem. Josephus, Jewish historian of the first century, identifies these people with the Scythians. Other later nonbiblical books believe the people Ezekiel was speaking of were from Ethiopia. It is best to consider Gog and Magog completely symbolic terms referring to evil that is always at war with God's children.

The New Jerusalem
Revelation 21

What does John mean by "a new heaven and a new earth"? The new heaven and new earth was mentioned by Peter (2 Peter 3:13) when he said, "We are looking forward to a new heaven and a new earth, the home of righteousness." Peter tells about the present earth and heaven being destroyed by fire. This could be what John means. Since John is talking in symbols, he may be describing the quality of life, of goodness and peace, of righteousness and purity. This seems to be the import of the scripture from 2 Peter also. Verses 3 and 4 of chapter 21 seem to verify this idea: "God himself will be with them and be their God. He will wipe every tear from their eyes. There will be no more death or mourning or crying or pain, for the old order of things has passed away.." The new heaven and new earth are apparently not so much a place as a condition. The entire context seems to imply this. "He who overcomes will inherit all this" (v 7). One can get this without money or without price. And what is the heritage? Apparently living in the new heaven and new earth, which means being children of God (v 7), enjoying God's presence (vv 3–4).

One of the seven angels then comes and shows John the bride, the wife of the Lamb. What did the angel show John? He showed John "the Holy City, Jerusalem, coming down out of heaven from God" (v 10). This cannot be a literal city. It would be impossible. Notice its dimensions: fifteen hundred miles long, fifteen hundred miles wide, and fifteen hundred miles high. Although this is an impossible situation, it probably fits John's Apocalyptic symbolism, because it is a perfect cube. John is still speaking in symbols. Although we may sing of streets of gold and jasper walls, John is using every possible word to try to describe the beauty of the church. This was what his suffering contemporaries needed, a high self-image. The evil government and society had made the Christians mud under their feet. The beautiful city probably included the church on earth, as Paul did in Galatians 4:26, and its final consummation at the end of the age.

To Christians, eternity and time are fused together, for even in this time world, "the glory of God" is the light and the Lamb is the lamp (Rev 21:23). In the beautiful church, the true church, "nothing impure will ever enter it, nor will anyone who does what is shameful or deceitful, but only those whose names are written in the Lamb's book of life" (v 27). The Lord is the light and they reign forever and ever (22:5). In Revelation 1:6, John had already said that Christians were made a kingdom of priests to God, and in 5:10, they reign both here and hereafter. What a comfort it must have been to Christians persecuted to death by an evil kingdom to discover that they were reigning, that they were part of an eternal kingdom that death could not destroy. To see themselves as the beautiful city must have been more than comfort. What it must have meant to their self-image, their self-respect, their whole view and concept of Christianity!

Although we do not have the key to the code or the symbols John used, we can still see how fitting those symbols were. The walls of the city would give protection. The light of the city was like the light of a stone most precious. Its foundations included the prophets or Old Testament and the apostles of the New Testament. The building was jasper with streets of pure gold.

John apparently goes to the limits of his vocabulary trying to describe the beautiful church, the bride of the Lamb, the holy city of Jerusalem coming down out of heaven from God. Perhaps we need more persons like John to visualize again the beauty of Christ's bride. Usually performance does not exceed the dream preceding it. If we see ourselves as part of the church, pure and spotless, we may just become pure and spotless. But if we think the church is a group of imperfect, unholy, unwise, frivolous, or frustrated people, that is very much what she is apt to become.

10
THE EPILOGUE AND CONCLUSION

Revelation 22:6–21

The Apocalypse ends with several important statements that have formed the bulwark of the church for generations. First, the words are trustworthy and true. As Isaiah had said many years before, "The grass withers and the flowers fall, but the word of our God stands forever" (Is 40:8). A blessing is pronounced by John on those who keep the prophecy of the book (Rev 22:7). No one was to add to or take from these words (vv 18–19). It is true and has always been true that the word of God stands forever. This is what John proclaims, and this is an important principle for the church to remember.

Apocalyptic writings were often sealed or hidden from view and waited until a future time to be revealed. John's prophecy is not to be sealed because it is soon to be fulfilled. The facts were that John was already a victim of the persecution, and at least one other Christian was mentioned as already martyred (2:13), and far worse things were very soon to happen to the entire church.

The threat of punishment does not always bring about change of character. The evildoers will still do evil, John says, and the righteous still will be righteous (v 11).

The message is from Jesus, the foundation of the church. He is called the Alpha and the Omega, the first and the last letters of the Greek alphabet. He is the first and the last, and all judgment is in his hands. He is also called the root and offspring of David. Verse 16 is a fulfillment of Isaiah 11:1.

Verses 17 and 18 give an invitation to all who are thirsty to come and partake of the water of life without price. The book ends with the phrase that was possibly a usual ending to first-century prayers, "Come, Lord Jesus." The phrase is used by Paul in 1 Corinthians 16:22.

Unfortunately, in our time, being a Christian is still something of which to be proud. One can scarcely run for office without saying one belongs to a certain church. To be a Sunday school teacher is to have a much better chance in the election. The end result of this is that many who call themselves Christians live on a low level, attempting to see how close they can get to sin and still be Christian. This is wholly out of character with what the true church is to be. The true church, the bride of Christ, is pure and spotless, drawing its morality and its strength from the One who sits on the throne. The more one can see of him, the less attractive the world is. The Apocalypse gives many pictures of him and of the church. In the Apocalypse the church stood against evil, the martyrs overcame Satan by the blood of the Lamb, and the word of their testimony, knowing it would mean death. They stood against the imperial cult in spite of economic, social, and cultural deprivations. Finally, many gave their very lives.

The church, as it enters the twenty-first century, needs to rediscover its character and its destiny. How like John's picture of the beautiful city are Paul's words to the Ephesians in Ephesians 2:19–21:

> You are no longer foreigners and aliens, but fellow citizens with God's people and members of God's household, built on the foundation of the apostles and prophets, with Christ Jesus himself as the chief cornerstone. In him the

10 THE EPILOGUE AND CONCLUSION

whole building is joined together and rises to become a holy temple in the Lord.

That was the character of the church of the first century.

Because of its infinite relationship with God, it was the light of the world, a city that was set on a hill that could not be hid. It was never meant to copy the world or be led by the world in any way. It was to be a light, pure and spotless, shining most brightly in the darkest places. When crime increases and evil abounds, one wonders if the church has fully realized its destiny. The Apocalypse brings us face to face with the real issues, the constant war between good and evil, between Satan and God. It is a battle that will last until the end of time. The invitation to be on the right side is set before us. The final result is also made clear. The vision of Christ in his final triumph is given again and again. The church is shown strong and able to withstand the evil forces. All of these things the modern church needs. We need the constant repetition John gives. How sad that the message has been lost because of quibbling over the symbols that were mainly the sound effects and furniture, the backdrop of the major drama. It is sad because we never stand alone. Each of us has an influence on someone, somewhere. These are made better or worse by the word of our testimony, our lives lived before them. That word is dulled into insignificance, unless we have been "washed by the blood of the Lamb." These two characteristics made the church what it was. We, too, can overcome by the blood of the Lamb and the word of our testimony. The world has not changed much in two thousand years. The same temptations, perhaps under different symbols, faces every child of God in every century. At such times, it is good to know that Christ himself gives the invitation to partake of the water of life freely. This must have been Paul's feeling when just before his death he wrote, "Now there is in store for me the crown of righteousness, which the Lord, the righteous Judge, will award to me on that day—and not only to me, but also to all who have longed for his appearing" (2 Timothy 4:8). If this is our lifestyle, we can all say joyfully with John, "Amen, come Lord Jesus."

Appendix A
Glossary of Symbols

Angels: Usually messengers.
Armageddon: (Rev 16) Symbolic city depicting the battle between good and evil.
Babylon: Ancient symbol for Rome. Note 1 Peter 5:13.
The beast: The Roman Empire, personified by the Emperor Domitian.
The second beast: Imperial cult.
The Book or Scroll: Quite frequently in Apocalyptic, e.g., Ezekiel is told to eat the book (3:1), as is John in Revelation 10:8–10. Possibly symbolic of the love for God's word and the secrecy of its message.
Clothed in white: Possibly a symbol for the Christians in heaven. Also means purity of heart.
The dragon: Satan.
The four corners of the earth: Universal, worldwide.
The four winds: Judgment.
Harlotry: Idol worship.
Mark of the beast: The mark on the right hand or the forehead shows its visibility. The mark was a visible sign that the person was a follower of the imperial cult. The "mark" may have been a certificate of worship or membership.[1] It may have been some kind of brand such as was used for slaves[2] or "undoubtedly figurative."[3] The passage is definitely a reference to a required allegiance to the worship of the emperor.
Seven: Meaning complete, whole, no limit.
Seals: Hidden, a mystery that can be revealed only by God. The book is sealed until God makes it known to his messenger, John.

---

1. Morris, *Revelation of St. John*, 173.
2. Ford, *Revelation*, 215.
3. Kiddle, *Revelation*, 258.

A COMMONSENSE APPROACH TO...REVELATION

Throne in heaven: God's dwelling place; or God's ownself.

The twelve tribes of Israel: The universal church. Israel or the word *Jew* is used for Christian by Paul in Romans 2:28–29 and Galatians 4:21–31.

The woman clothed with the sun (Rev 12:1): The church. This figure is used for the church in other passages, such as Galatians 4:26 and Isaiah 66:7. Her child represents the new converts. The pain at childbirth is the concern of the church for lost humanity. This, also mentioned in Isaiah (66:8), is essential to the birth of others into the kingdom of God.

The woman arrayed in purple and scarlet or the harlot (17:1–6) is another figure for Babylon or the ancient symbol for Rome.

Appendix B
Recapitulation Defined and Illustrated

Recapitulation is a dramatic method of presentation that gradually increases its impact. It repeats or retells a message, each time with new characters or symbols. The central message remains the same. Revelation, chapters 6 through 22, follows this method in a series of four presentations, all with the same point: God is victorious over all the forces (and faces) of evil and the church will endure. The Alpha and Omega is coming to judge (Rev 1:7–8; 22:12–13). Not only do we want to be on the side of the triumphant Christ, but we live with the hope that our suffering in the battle between good and evil will be answered by the one who "will wipe every tear from [our] eyes" (21:4). We will then belong with the one who makes all things new! Amen. Come, Lord Jesus.

Chapter 1–5 Introductory

Series I

Chapter 6: The white horse is an invasion of the Roman Empire, which was followed by the red horse or civil strife. Famine, pestilence, and death are symbolized by other horsemen. The black horse is literal famine. All of this is a judgment on the Roman Empire for persecution of the Christians. Chapter 7 The Christians are protected from these calamities because they are sealed. A description of their future hope is also given.

Series II

Chapters 8–11: Covers the same material as above but under different symbols. The church will endure.

Series III

Chapters 12–13: The conflict of the early church with paganism (the dragon) and with the imperial cult set up to enforce emperor worship.

Chapter 14: This passage shows the victory of God which is given to encourage the church.

Chapter 15–16: Continuation of judgment of the Roman Empire.

Chapter 17–19: Judgment on the great city of Rome (Babylon). Christians are to have nothing to do with paganism (to come out of Babylon).

Series IV

Chapters 20–22: Conflict with Satan and the final victory of good over evil.

The above is adapted from *The Revelation of John* by Shirley Jackson Case and *Studies in the New Testament* by Otto E Linn.

Appendix C
Satan Cast Out Revelation 12:7–12

There is much interest today in Satan. Some worship him, some fear him, and many misunderstand the scriptures relating to him. One of the most misunderstood is Revelation 12:7–12. The text says Satan was thrown down to earth and his angels thrown down with him. The text is in apocalyptic language and should not be taken literally, just as other texts in the book should not be taken literally.

There are schools of thought that insist that Satan once lived in heaven but was cast out. This may be true, but there is no scripture except this symbolic one to prove this point. To use symbolic language literally is to misinterpret the writer and his time. It is very uncomfortable to feel that Satan once lived in heaven and was cast out. If he was cast out, we might be cast out. So where is our security?

Another text often used to prove Satan's being cast out of heaven is found in Isaiah 14. The specific text is verse 12, which says, "How you are fallen from heaven, O Day Star, son of Dawn!" (NRSV). The Authorized or King James has "Lucifer" rather than "Day Star." The problem is not the difference in these two versions of the name. The problem is that the scripture is often taken out of context. The entire passage is addressed to the king of Babylon, as is evident from reading verse 4: "You will take up this taunt against the king of Babylon" (NRSV).

Another scripture often used with the Isaiah and Revelation texts is in Luke 10:18, where Jesus says to the disciples, "I saw Satan fall like lightning from heaven." There is no way to determine whether Jesus is talking about the speed with which Satan travels or is speaking in literal terms about an incident that he witnessed.

It is wiser to use proper methods of interpretation and not yield to the temptation to take scriptures out of context to prove some theological point. In the book of Revelation,

A COMMONSENSE APPROACH TO...REVELATION

John is discussing the Roman Empire and the evil powers that are motivating it. By divine revelation John sees the demise of that empire and the ultimate defeat of evil. That issue becomes greatly clouded when one goes off in fanciful interpretations about the devil.

Bruce, F. F. *New Testament History*. New York: Doubleday, 1969.

Calkins, Raymond. *The Social Message of the Apocalypse*. New York: Womans Press, 1920.

Case, Shirley Jackson. *The Revelation of John*. Chicago: University of Chicago Press, 1919.

Charles, R. H. *Studies in the Apocalypse*. Edinburgh: T & T Clark, 1915.

———. The International Critical Commentary. 2 volumes. New York: Scribner's, 1920.

Ford, J. Massyngberde. *Revelation*. The Anchor Bible. New York: Doubleday, 1975.

Kiddle, Martin. *The Revelation of St. John*. The Moffatt New Testament Commentary. New York: Harper, 1940.

Linn, Otto F. *Hebrews to Revelation*. Vol. 3, *Studies in the New Testament*. Anderson, IN: privately printed, [1942].

Metzger, Bruce M. *Breaking the Code: Understanding the Book of Revelation*. Nashville: Abingdon Press, 1993.

Morris, Leon. *The Revelation of St. John*. The Tyndale New Testament Commentaries. Grand Rapids, MI: Eerdmans, 1969.

Porter, Frank C. *The Message of the Apocalyptical Writers*. New York: Scribner's, 1916.

Rist, Martin. "Revelation." In *The Interpreter's Bible*, edited by George Arthur Buttrick, 12:347–613. Nashville, TN: Abingdon, 1957.

Scott, E. P. *The Book of Revelation*. New York: Scribner's, 1940.

Study Guide

TO THE GROUP LEADER

You have taken on an ambitious project—that of helping your students come to appreciate and understand the book of the New Testament that has been treated most often as a "sideshow" in the church. The bizarre effect of the text and the emotive power of the great themes of conflict of the book of Revelation has titillated and obsessed some, has offended others, and has confused most of its readers. Strong's commonsense approach restores John's Revelation to its proper place in the church—a dramatic presentation of God's triumph over all the forces and faces of evil, and a compelling exhortation to the church to "keep the faith," especially in the face of despair.

Begin your group study by asking that those present express their experiences with this book. Expect strong emotional responses from some who may have invested a good deal of energy in the text. Expect discomfort and anxiety from others. Offer this study as a means for reclaiming the value of this book in your congregation and for the Christian life. Set up some guidelines that will help to create confidence and comfort in this study. The following are suggestions:

1. Give the perspective that all are going on a spiritual pilgrimage. "Let us all make this quest together, fresh, and as if we have never been on this path before. Let us agree not to state any final conclusions until we have all completed this journey together. Let us agree to grant Dr. Strong the role of tour guide."
2. Request that God will guide your minds and hearts in understanding and applying the great truths of this book,

the legacy of your forefathers and mothers who received this hope-filled word from John in the midst of their suffering and confusion—and who have passed the book on to you.
3. Encourage open questions and dialogue.
4. Exhort personal commitment to apply the wisdom of this book of the Bible to personal and congregational life.

How to Study the Book of Revelation as a Group:

1. Read the whole book through as a dramatic reading. It would be best to read it through in one reading. Since it will take about ninety minutes to read, you will either have to create special time or plan for two sessions to be involved in the presentation.

    If possible, break the reading down into parts. For example, in chapter one, a narrator can read the prologue (vv 1–3); "John" can read 1:4–7, 9–11, 12–17; the "Lord God" can read 1:8; the "Son of Man" can read 1:11 and 1:17–20. For chapter two through three, seven persons can read the letters to the seven churches. Tell those participating in the presentation that they cannot overdramatize this book!

2. Study Dr. Strong's book through, one chapter per week. Encourage group members to reread the major sections of Revelation being covered for the week before they study Dr. Strong's chapter. Prepare readers each week to read the portions of the text being referred to in the chapter when the class comes to them. Give adult readers time to read short sections of the chapters in Dr. Strong's book. Raise the questions or discussion topics offered in this guide.

STUDY QUESTIONS

Chapter One

1. Begin by asking three readers to read 1:12–16; 6:1–8; and 12:1–6 aloud for the group.

2. Which opinions have you heard about of the four categories Dr. Strong has identified (Futurist, Preterist, etc)?

3. What do you think about the diversity of opinion about how the book of Revelation is to be understood? Should Christians just give up trying to study this book? Should leaders of the church just teach one of the opinions? Should adult students be told about all of the opinions?

4. What does Dr. Strong offer as the way to discover how we should try to understand this Bible book?

5. What other books in the Bible are written like the book of Revelation. Why are these books written in symbols or codes?

6. What does the word Apocalypse mean? What was the purpose for the writing of Apocalypses?

7. Why does Dr. Strong say that "we should not look for historical accuracy in such books"?

8. What is the "core or kernel of truth" in apocalyptic writing?

9. Why has the book of Revelation been the favorite of people in concentration camps? Would this book help you if you or your loved ones were suffering?

10. Memorize the four major ideas in apocalyptic literature.

A COMMONSENSE APPROACH TO…REVELATION

11. Who was persecuting Christians when John sent Revelation to them?

12. Why were the early Christians thought to be "atheists"?

13. Does Dr. Strong's chapter help you? Do you think it is important to understand the historical situation that God inspired John to respond to? Does historical information help this book and its methods make more sense to you?

Chapter Two

1. What gives the book of Revelation "eternal authority"?

2. Why did John write to only seven churches in Asia?

3. What was the problem at Ephesus? Do you see any signs of this problem in your life or in your congregation?

4. What does John mean by "Jews" in the address to Smyrna?

5. Would the words to Smyrna comfort you if you were imprisoned or even martyred by your faith. Would you "keep the faith"? What statements are the same in Christ's words to Philadelphia?

6. Why is the church at Pergamum in trouble? What instruction is given to them? Is the instruction important for you? For your congregation?

7. Thyatira is guilty of the same failure as Pergamum? Should the whole congregation be held responsible for the deeds of some in the congregation? What correctives does this text offer for the deceiver and the deceived at Thyatira?

8. How are the churches of Sardis and Laodicea similar? In what ways does John's description of their failure remind

you of your congregation? Would John's instruction to those congregations help your congregation? How? What about you as a part of your congregation? Where do you stand?

9. Which churches do you want your congregation to be modeled after?

10. What questions come to you after studying the letters to the churches? What do you wish you could know more about?

Chapter Three

1. What does the door in heaven symbolize? Of what do John's words "I was in the Spirit" (4:2) remind you?

2. What is the focus of all of chapter 4 of the book of Revelation? Hint: what symbol in verse two is repeated throughout the chapter?

3. Can you participate in the worship of the living creatures, the elders, and then the angels by singing songs that use phrases from the praises in 4:8; 4:11; 5:9; and 5:12?

4. List all the symbols used to define Christ in Revelation 5. Recall what each symbol represents.

5. Dr. Strong has pointed out the inclusiveness of Christ's work: people from every tribe, language, and nation have "been purchased" and so are a part of God's kingdom and serve God as priests. How are you doing at reflecting God's work in Christ in your community?

6. This vision of heavenly worship was granted to John for what reason? How does this scene affect you?

Chapter Four

1. Think of the military imagery of the four horses, their riders, and the implements they carry. Think of the history of Rome and their military equipment. What images today would be used to create the same dread that these images caused the readers of AD 81–96.

2. What comfort was offered to the church of John's time with the symbols of the four horsemen? How can the destiny of Rome affect the way we look at political events and the affairs of nations today?

3. When the fifth seal was opened the scroll revealed the vivid picture of the souls under the altar. What did this picture mean and how does it help you?

4. Read the "Little Apocalypse" in Matthew 24; Luke 21; and Mark 13. Write a list of the cosmic events that represent God's judgment. List the earthly events.

5. How would this picture of God's wrath comfort the church in its Lime of great suffering?

6. Are the "four corners of the earth" meant to be geographical points on the map representing that the earth is flat and angular?

7. Look up the lists of the twelve tribes of Israel in the Old Testament. In Genesis 35:25, Dan is listed instead of Manasseh, who appears in Revelation. Metzger explains the fact that the tribe of Dan is excluded in this way: "The tribe of Dan is not mentioned perhaps because of the tradition that the Antichrist would arise from this tribe. The tradition may have had its source in Genesis 49:17 (compare the omission of the same tribe from 1 Chronicles 4–7). The total of twelve tribes is maintained by replacing the name

of Joseph with the names of his two sons, Ephraim and Manasseh."[1]

8. Copy down the words quoted from Revelation 7:15–16 (beginning with "he who sits on the throne") to send to someone you know is suffering. Create a song based upon these beautiful words.

Chapter Five

1. When the seventh seal is opened, we might expect another great and tumultuous scene. Instead there is silence. The effect of the silence is to increase the tension for the next series of God's judgments, each one announced by a trumpet. Notice what happened immediately after the silence—worship consisting of the prayers of all the saints that rise up before God, as if lifting on the perfumed smoke of the incense. Incense was used in the worship of God in the Jerusalem temple (destroyed in AD 70). What part do you think the prayers play in the next series of calamities.

2. Compare the vivid sounds and sights of John's vision with modern action movies. If this vision had been meant to be taken literally and the terror of it could be depicted in high-definition with surround sound, what rating would the movie be given for its violence quotient? Remember 9:6.

3. What are the four main points of this series?

4. Look up Appendix B for an overview of recapitulation.

5. The numbers in 11:2–3, forty-two months or 1260 days, can also be expressed as three and a half years. This period of time is the apocalyptic symbol for the "abomination that

---

1. Metzger, *Breaking the Code*, 60.

desolates." See Daniel 9:27 and 12:7, which refers to the historical desecration of the Jerusalem temple by the Syrian general Antiochus IV from 167 to 164 BC. An idol was set up in God's temple and the foreign soldiers committed indecent acts inside the temple. No worship of God was allowed. That awful event became the symbol of utter horror for the Jewish people and also the early Christians.

6. Think of how your congregation would feel if vandals defaced your sanctuary, set up a statue of something that opposed the true God, and acted in immoral ways to ridicule the worship of God. What if you were powerless to change such a reality?

7. The word *Gentiles* refers to pagans or non-Christians who will torment the church. *Temple* refers to the church, which means the people of God (see 1 Corinthians 3:16; 1 Peter 2:5; Ephesians 2:21). There was an inscription on the wall of the outer court of the Jerusalem temple, the court the Gentiles were restricted to, which threatened them with death if they dared to enter the court of the Jews. That is the wall that Paul preached about: "For he himself [Jesus Christ] is our peace, who has made the two one [Jews and Gentiles] and has destroyed the barrier, the dividing wall of hostility" (Eph 2:14). Find a map of the temple in the back of a Bible or in a Bible dictionary or atlas.

8. John is emphasizing that even when the church's lot is to suffer persecution at the hands of the world, it continues to be faithful. The resurrection of the two witnesses is a sign of hope. The church, appearing to be defeated, also will be resurrected by the sovereign act of God. Think of a place around the globe in the last fifty years where it appeared that the church was defeated. What has happened? Recall a time when it appeared to you (and to others) that the church or your congregation was dead and disgraced. How did God

bring new life and even honor to that experience?

9. The last trumpet call (Rev 11:15) transports us to the heavenly scene. Part of the scene is the "ark of his covenant" (11:19), which was a sign of God's presence with his people in the Old Testament. The heavenly chorus sings victory. This could have been the end of John's book. But John's presentation is not done. It is to repeat again the same sort of pictures and teachings with another set of woes.

Chapter Six

1. Dr. Strong explains that the woman is to be understood as the church. Another interpretation is that the woman is Mary, who has the male child Jesus, who is to "rule all the nations with an iron scepter" (12:5). Support for that interpretation is that Psalm 2, which was a prophecy of the Messiah, is the source for these words (2:9). Revelation 12:5 would then be a reference to Christ's ascension. Revelation 12:17 signifies the war of Satan against the church ("the rest of her offspring"). It is possible that the woman is a "personification of the ideal community of God's people, first in its Jewish form, in which Mary gave birth to Jesus the Messiah, and then in its Christian form, in which it was persecuted by a political power as evil as the dragon (12:6)."[2] As you engage in this exercise, notice that you are doing what Dr. Strong has taught you so far in this book. You are looking for the best "commonsense" answer to the puzzles of a code book. Congratulations for entering the dialogue!

2. "I will build my church and the powers of death shall not prevail against it" (see Matt 16:18). Jesus has given the church this promise. List the powers of death you see

---

2. Metzger, *Breaking the Code*, 74.

facing the church, at least those of which you are aware. What about your congregation. List them all. Now after each one, write in "shall not prevail" or "cannot win."

3. In Revelation 12:11, Satan is overcome "by the blood of the Lamb and the word of their [Christian] testimony." Dr. Strong defines testimony as more than words: "It is mainly life lived under fire." Where are you "under fire" in your life? How are you tempted? Remember times you have overcome the temptation to compromise your testimony. Dr. Strong says that each time, you have thrown Satan down. May you be encouraged to persevere!

4. Memorize the beautiful promise of Isaiah 43:2–3.

5. Practice "sorrow for sinful humanity." Become aware of "spiritual warfare" in your community. What can you do to support the force of good in that battle? Devote some of your energy to that good!

6. What do you think about Dr. Strong's emphasis on non-retaliation in the face of persecution? If a Domitian figure with all his forces threatened death if you refused to compromise your faith, what would you do?

7. You have probably heard much about the number 666 in popular Christian culture. Dr. Metzger gives us an expanded statement that supports Dr. Strong's analysis:

> The number "six hundred sixty-six" is, in the first place, a symbol of the greatest imperfection, for it is the sacred number seven less one, repeated thrice. John says that it is a human number; that is, it is the number of a person's name. Now, in both the Greek and Hebrew alphabets, the letters also served as numerals, and it was a well-known technique to add up the letters that comprise a proper name. If we did that in

English, the number of a girl named Ada would be six. That is, A is the first letter of the alphabet and D is the fourth letter, and consequently the numerical equivalent of Ada is 1 + 4 + 1 = 6. Who is this satanic beast, symbolized by the number 666? Over the centuries a very great deal of ingenuity has been expended in attempting to answer this question. A further complication arises from the fact that some ancient manuscripts of the book of Revelation give the number 616 instead of 666.

Among the names and titles that have been proposed to solve the cryptogram, the most probable candidate is the Emperor Nero. If we add the numerical values in Hebrew spelling of the name Neron Caesar we obtain 666; on the other hand, since his name can be equally well be spelled without the last N, if we omit the final N, the total will be 616. There does not appear to be any other name, or a name with a title, that satisfies both 666 and 616.[3]

Now that you have heard the arguments of Drs. Strong and Metzger, what do you think of the statements you have heard about 666?

8. "Defile themselves with women" in 14:4 is language from the Old Testament where any involvement with idol worship was called "fornication" or "adultery." The 144,000 have not defiled themselves with emperor worship.

9. Next time you attend worship, remember reading about the torture of early Christians and give God praise for the freedom you now enjoy.

---

3. Metzger, *Breaking the Code*, 76.

Chapter Seven

1. This week, meet your problems by first praying to God and offering praise. Use the song of 15:3–4 to open your prayer.

2. Think of references you have heard to a battle at Armageddon. It is usually identified as Megiddo, the name of a city and the pass nearby, which was a place where many ancient battles were fought (Judges 5:19–21). John uses this familiar reference to symbolize a great battle between good and evil. Evil will be conquered; Jesus Christ will triumph (19:13). Some Christians think this refers to a future battle that will literally be fought in the plains of Megiddo. They think of literal armies and armaments. What do you think of Dr. Strong's warning that John was writing symbolically so that church would be encouraged with the news that Rome would fall? If you are having difficulty with the idea that it is best to understand this material as symbolic, see the descriptions of Jesus again throughout this book. Are we to think literally of Jesus as a sheep? Or as a lion? Does Jesus carry a sickle or the modern equivalent of a weed-whacker as pictured in 14:14?

3. Have you ever wondered why art has so often portrayed angels or saints with harps? Notice 15:2. Even today harp music is thought to be the most restful of all by many music critics.

4. Notice that despite the plagues, "they refused to repent" (16:9–11). The point being made here and in 14: 10–11 is not that God is vindictive and sadistic. The author continues to use symbolic language to express the fate of those who continuously reject God. Those who choose to participate on the side of evil, no matter how innocent it may seem, turn away from the God of good and love. Such a choice

has a "forever and ever" quality (14:11) as God respects the free will he has granted to each of us. Metzger reminds us that the power of choice is behind these scenes of judgment: "the sufferings of those who persist in rejecting God's love in Christ as self-imposed and self-perpetuated."[4]

Chapter Eight

1. The ancient city of Rome was built on seven hills (see 17:7 and 9). Its population at the time of the emperor Augustus was about one million and by the time of the emperor Trajan was two million. The city was renowned for its sights, its buildings, and for being "the center of the world." Given her great power (see 18:18), and the cruelties endured at her hands, it is no wonder that John spends two chapters defining her fate.

2. What is the major theme of Revelation 17?

3. Notice the imports of Rome listed in 18:11–15. They are typical of that day, including slaves (the end of verse 13).

4. Read Jeremiah 50 and compare it to Revelation 18.

5. "Come out from her, my people" is a call to the church. In John's writing it was a warning to avoid any association with the imperial cult (emperor worship). What kinds of gods does the church fraternize with today? What warning does God call us with today? Of what does the church need to "come out" today?

---

4. Metzger, *Breaking the Code*, 79.

Chapter Nine

1. Memorize the word *hallelujah*. The next time you hear the word or sing the word in worship remember not only its meaning but also that you join in the praise of the people of God that has spanned centuries.

2. Read Luke 12:35–38. In what ways does the church need to prepare so that she is ready for the groom? In what ways do you "watch" so that you will not miss the "party"?

3. Dr. Strong points out that the picture of Jesus in Revelation 19:11–16 is not that of a literal warlord leading a literal army who maims and kills and leaves a feast for vultures. Many Christians find this image to be at odds with Jesus' teachings, particularly Matthew 5:38–48 and Luke 6:27–36 (which Paul refers to in Romans 12 and concludes with the words "Overcome evil with good"). What do you think?

4. When faced with no reason to hope on earth, what hope does John offer the Christians of his time? What is the hope you "hang on to"?

5. Memorize Romans 8:31–37.

6. Summarize the premillennial view in your own words.

7. Summarize the nonmillennial view in your own words.

8. What do the Gospels teach us about the kingdom of God?

9. What are the major points of Dr. Strong's presentation about Revelation 20? List them. Does her argument make "sense" to you?

10. Memorize Revelation 21:3-4. How does this passage help you?

STUDY GUIDE

Chapter Ten

1. In what way does the book of Revelation represent the church? How does your local church measure up to that picture?

2. From where does the church draw its morality and strength?

3. Apply biblical truths to your own identity as a Christian. What have you learned or remembered as you have read chapter ten of Dr. Strong's book that you needed right now in your life?

4. Dr. Strong says, "The Apocalypse brings us face to face with the real issues." What are the real issues?

5. List the ways this study of the book of Revelation has strengthened you in your faith and in your part of being "the church."

6. Some people spend a majority of their energy and attention on arguing a particular interpretation of the book of Revelation and its application to the events of this time. Evaluate the percentage of the New Testament that presents apocalyptic material or information about the "end time." Perhaps that percentage should direct the amount of attention Christians and the church should spend on such presentations. What do you think?

7. If we are to spend only a small percentage of our time on concerns about the "end time," what should we do with the rest of our strength? Read Acts 1:6–11.

8. What is the most important understanding this study has given you? Write a statement summarizing your most helpful learning experiences.

About the Author

A native of Loup County, Nebraska, Marie Strong was an ordained minister in the Church of God and served the church as Bible professor at Anderson College for twenty-eight years. In addition, she pastored churches and taught at Warner Pacific College, Gardner Bible College, Anderson University, and the School of Theology, and in public schools.

Before entering her career in education, Strong was a pastor in Nebraska and was widely known for her Christian writings. Two of her most prominent efforts were *The Spirit and Method of Altar Work* and *Basic Teachings from Patmos*. At her death, Strong was working on a revision of this latter book under the title *A Commonsense Approach to the Book of Revelation*.

To many in the Church of God, her lasting contributions may be in the field of active Christian service. She founded and sponsored Christianity in Action on the Anderson College campus, which evolved into the widely acclaimed Tri-S (originally Student Summer Service and now Study, Serve, Share) program. She was also the founder of the downtown Anderson Christian center, a community shelter for homeless people.

Marie's ministry began with humble and rigorous service. In her own words, "my first pastorate was a tiny rural congregation. It was 1934 and well into the Great Depression. Drought had hit the area, dust storms were frequent, and money was a memory."

She left her pastoral work to attend Anderson College in 1941. She got a job with Delco Remy of Anderson and worked seven nights a week while attending classes during the day. After graduation in 1945, she was asked by Adam Miller to teach in summer school at the college. Twenty-eight years of teaching Bible subjects in the college followed.

"Upon retirement in 1978," Marie remembers, "I decided to spend time in churches, teaching, preaching, and leading retreats." Soon after her retirement, she sustained a return of the stomach ailment that had plagued her for years. In Pinecrest, Kentucky, enduring the pain while leading a women's conference, she asked for prayer for her condition. The women surrounded her and prayed. "The Lord healed me instantly," Marie recalls. "I went from the room to the lunch table and ate food I had been unable to eat for years, with no ill effects." She summarized her ministry in the latter years: "The great miracle of God's love has enabled me to work in the churches unhindered by dietary regulations or pain. God has been wonderfully good to me in every way." She died in January 1995 at her home in Pendleton, Indiana.

James Earl Massey officiated at her funeral at Park Place Church of God, Anderson, Indiana. In addition, six friends shared remembrances of their relationships with Strong. Juanita Leonard referred to Strong's early Christian days: "Marie didn't own a Bible but borrowed one from her brother. She was so excited about God that she wanted to gulp down everything at one time. She wore that Bible out the first year."

Lloyd Lambert, of the Christian Center in Anderson, testified of her: "She was mentor, confidante, guide, always there with her gracious acceptance and uplifting spirit."

Norman Beard, who directed the Tri-S program at Anderson University, said, "I think if we were to honor Marie most we would recommit out lives to humble service to the least of these."

ABOUT THE AUTHOR

Marie Strong: Scholar and Teacher
A Tribute presented at the funeral of Marie Strong, January 23, 1995

Since the war years of the 1940s, the Anderson University campus has known and learned from Marie Strong. First she was an Anderson College student. Then, just as the school was first being accredited in 1946, she began her distinguished teaching career. With soldiers home, now armed with the GI Bill instead of rifles, the Anderson College faculty had to grow along with the growing student body. Marie was off to the University of Chicago to expand her learning in order to enhance her coming teaching career

Soon armed with doctoral studies, she was back in Anderson, ready to grow with the school and be serious about teaching the Bible. Over the following years, Professor Strong would come to represent the best of what it meant for a young college to be accredited as a quality place to learn. Earlier she had been a pastor, a pioneer who traveled often on horseback in less than ideal circumstances. Now there were academic trails to travel. The nurturing pastor was still part of who she was; but now ministry would happen amid the rigors of the classroom.

The Department of Religious Studies of Anderson University, her home base for a long time, includes today five members who were first helped to find their way under her instruction and a fifth who was privileged to start his career as her teaching assistant. Marie was a mentor, an affirmer, an inspirer. If you were lazy, you were in trouble in her class. If you were willing to work, whatever your ability level, she would gladly help bring out the best in you. Her standards were high; after all, the subject was the Word of God and the issues in question were the stuff of life itself.

Recalls one of her former students, now himself a widely recognized biblical scholar: "She shaped me when I was just beginning. She knew the biblical text well and wouldn't let students avoid it. She insisted on raising critical questions about proper biblical interpretation and made clear that the issues were not being made up by alien unbelievers, but emerged right out of the texts themselves. She did not 'mother' students with a shallow sentimentalism that tried to pass for adequate academics. She was gentle, but in a firm and focused way that retained a student's dignity without undermining the expectation of excellence."

Marie was an instrument of the Spirit. God had inspired the biblical texts, she believed, and God wanted to inspire her students to probe these texts for life-changing meaning. Hers was a tough head and a warm heart, an ideal combination for a church-related college. She always believed that the altar of faith is as important as the reference desk of the library. To separate faith in church from reason in the classroom is to have lost one's way. Learning is for living; to know the Bible aright, according to Marie, is to be shaped and sent by it.

Marie Strong was both a minister and an academic. She loved the Sermon on the Mount material in Matthew's Gospel. There she watched Jesus link teaching, believing, and obeying. Therefore, as a student of Jesus, Marie consistently connected in her own teaching what the Bible says with how we actually are to act. Students should pray, she believed, and church people should think. All believers should serve.

She was a faithful daughter of the Church of God movement, heeding the call to go back to the Bible. Her love for the Scriptures was contagious. Being a scholar-teacher, she handled the theories and was careful with detail.

Marie Strong arrived on campus teaching, announcing, and modeling the meanings of the kingdom of God come neat in Christ. We who learned from her, and we are many, now carry a heavy responsibility to continue bearing the witness in thought and deed.

Barry L. Callen

www.ingramcontent.com/pod-product-compliance
Lightning Source LLC
Chambersburg PA
CBHW071833290426
44109CB00017B/1809